A.K.A. Peter Coco

The Feast of Saint Rocco

Memoir in Recipe, Story & Poem

Peter Cocuzza

VAGABOND

Published by VAGABOND
Mark Lipman, editor

VAGABOND

Intellectual Property
Cocuzza, Peter
The Feast of Saint Rocco
1st ed. / p.cm.

ISBN13: 978-1-936293-41-4

Made in the USA.

8/2020

This Book
IS ALSO DEDICATED
TO THOSE who, By
SIEGE OR By FAMINE
WATCH THEIR children
DIE IN THEIR ARMS
AND ON THEIR STREETS.

To Marilyn, my golden partner
since first rough draft days.

TABLE OF CONTENTS

PRELUDE

"Hey, that kid must be Autistic," I hear her say.

A young man, up on a strip-mall bench, legs folded lotus-like, hands rolled together into crotch – rocking like a clock – back and forth quickly – with a most serious look on his face, chewing his tongue with each push forward – eyes locked in a trance of repetition and need...seeing him, I recognize myself every day until puberty and first recognize that I had been through something stark and stigmatic...and just never looked back.

Through the 1950's, when the families convened on Sundays, sat around the living room perimeter in straight-back chairs, sofas and armchairs – seems like every other week or so – who would come, buck naked spinning on all fours, to the middle of the floor, greeting them? – Peter.

I heard the word 'Autistic' exactly once – at the start of a new decade that kept me too busy surviving and moving to even think that I was *different*, or to put my childhood into any kind of context...or to let go of the hurt.

this poor kid
on a bench
in a strip-mall
on my 50th birthday
released me
to begin to begin
to understand
the exorcism of my experience
and the Person
of Forgiveness

Belated Greetings from Asbury Park

2

Youth Bathed In Youth
Quicker Than Memory

Conjured
Foot Bare
Warm Sand
Seal Of Sky
Rake Of Sun
Line Of Distance
Dare Of Tide
Head First
Stretch Splash
Under Summertime Screams
Jump Released
To Surface

Wet Skin
Glistened
Beside
Wonder
And
Desire

All –
Teaching In Dimension
Dimension Itself

Within Triptych
Of Time Past
And Passing
One Soul

The Box

"Eat Morbarik!"

I run to remember – to discover – along the mountain sunset, then up Chestnut Hill – finally from my place. I don't eat or drink anything but water all day, doing this recovery from a decade of skeleton dances in cocaine mazed Big-Ass Town Without Pity. As I run I invoke the Muslim greeting used at the end of Ramadan, "Eid Morbarik," that I have bastardized for my head as *"Eat Morbarik"* – **"Eat Spirit."**

Eat Morbarik! I gasp like a boxer in training to the top of the hill and back down around to town – breathing tight into the center of Faith – thought swinging hemisphere to hemisphere...

Eat Morbarik! I am quiet alone hermit delivering myself Free – but this time it's not so easy for the decay and shame...and I need to strip to see what clothes I wear and I don't really know if it will work...

Eat Morbarik! The same five miles the same 3,000 strides pressed into the footprints of the last time around.

Eat Spirit! By grace at the tail of a scream, I am generating peace moving along this boundary and at least have that to contemplate, as I enter, finished running, passing through a farm gate at the head of a long evergreen/blue arcade road...at its end, completely hidden in tall trees, is my shelter – a way way away hunk of Tibet, fixed complete with sky. From here I will not sleep 'til I awaken.

Leaving India for the West depressed me a little every day until I came to Woodstock. Here the trees are sisters to the forests above Dharamsala, teaching with the same nurture what must be a language lined up in great circles growing out of the earth. I breathe memories incubated, now complimented – shared with their wisdom.

One summer day just outside of K.B. Dharamsala, unannounced and uninvited, I strolled into the garden of a Tibetan monk a guy from Detroit said he lived in. Every flower, every leaf, every stone, every blade of grass rippled with hallucinogenic sensation, vibrating in exquisite gestation, titillating each step I took on the narrow lanes I quickly began to understand I did not belong on. I was intruding, like I had happened into a laboratory or a sanctuary where something *else* was going on, being cultivated or maybe preserved. The feeling of *Mind* encircled me, like I was being watched very closely. I started to feel uncomfortable and controlled. A small structure, camouflaged by its simplicity, appeared. Squatting into the low entrance, I could see that someone lived there. Up from a meditation mat behind a little altar scattered with holy objects – *all that is necessary* – food, water, utensil, pot, pan and burner, tea, incense, candle, book and clothing – *all* in arm's reach from lotus position. In that instant, in that very Sutra of the material world set in front of me, I realized what the word *rich* meant.

Decades have bequeathed that day an agony, as I experience again, making a living in America's carrot and stick culture – useless obsessions ever sprouting – dangled in grasping processions of enforced desire – every taker, billionaire to bum, consumed with *real* poverty. Maybe that's why so many who have journeyed to the other side – to India – come to Woodstock...to keep things in arm's reach.

I have been downtown here, inside for years, alone and dry, blocked and locked on feelings and places turned in spirals to fit neat in closed drawers of time. Next to my desk sits a case I have taken out of storage. It is filled with trinkets and scraps from around the world...old passports, address books, letters, a few photos, drawings and a hundred poems. I haven't looked at this stuff for years. Maybe I was just too busy...or maybe I was afraid I'd be haunted by the adventure, here reduced to a fading pile, dusty with the smell of old paper. At the top of the case is a shoebox I took from my mother's closet the day after she was buried. In it I found a few of my old report cards, a penmanship award from Grammar School, my Confirmation certificate and every letter and postcard I had written to her in ten years or so from San Francisco to Ceylon and back. It is the only thing I have left of her – *pieces of me.*

I pull an envelope from the middle of the box. I recognize it immediately from the last time I had seen it – while rifling through her bottom drawer when I was a seven year old, alone with my fear, paralyzing visions and constant precognitions – separated from her by the distance of abuse – separated from everyone else by my different thoughts and very different behavior – spinning on all fours – rocking in place every time I sat down anywhere and not speaking much - it is a plain white envelope, bubbled with years, marked, 'Peter's Veil.' In it is an old piece of skin. Thirty-eight years before, it was the diameter of a baseball and still had a good deal of white on its face. Now, its dark brown center has taken over half of the skin which has shrunk to the size of a silver dollar.

Pressing the edge of my Veil, moving it around the desk blotter like a Ouija. I feel a sense of *affirmation,* the same as when I found that piece of skin the first time – affirmation of something I have always known – the Veil was wrapped around my head to protect me before birth, guarding me then...guarding me still.

I pluck a blue aerogram from the box. It is from Puri. It must have arrived in America before I did and gotten filed there unopened. Scrawling tiny enough to fit volumes on each side, front and back of the fold up thin paper tablet, Puri greets me as always, "Fisherman," blesses, praises, then complains about the price of an egg, a liter of kerosene and a kilo of ghee, before updating on Samuel the tailor, Gustav in Japan, Ken and Barbara in Scotland, forwarding Martin, Leslie and Sachiko's new address in Tuscany and news of Mother feeling better, his son Cheecu back in grade school, as is daughter Neelam who sends love to her "Ja Jo" she now calls me...all before he blasts science as the source of modern misery as well as keeping me dialing the parchment in swirls following poetry inlaid on its perimeters:

> 1) "The Christ – The Buddha – The Child"
> with naked body/soul
> playing with sand
> shaping thoughts
> oblivious to the world around
> absorbed in himself

Knowing not of Void
of God
    The World below
    The World above
Living with his own thoughts.

2) I know of an ancient bearded beggar
   with his paper bowl begging of all
   begging of me
           me myself
           begging of "Him"

   are we not beggars both?

3) I sought my love in the lonely jungle,
   but the thorns turned me away

   in the dark waters of the pond
   the fish were the only ones
   on top of the mountain
   the clouds stared me down
         and yet I found my love
         within this hollow body

      I was drunk with joy
      My quest is fulfilled,
      after all.

    ... ...

I remember him that first day, breezing across the room of his Post House Haven – 'Neelam's Café Espresso Bar' – Zorba sprung in Urdu – arms wide open, spinning his web. Vittorio De Sica, sprinkled with a generous hit of Ramakrishna acting out an 'Almost Grown' Ken Kesey – retracing his precocious chameleon for each comer – each sojourner – each wanderer to his audience. Neelam returns from school with a lame rabbit she has found grazing in the fields of wild ganja behind the shop. Cheecu shimmies up a 50 foot tree and fetches some special fruit his father has promised the beautiful blonde from Colorado who always stops to see him on her way back up to McCloud Ganj, where she studies Tibetan. Could Cheecu run down to the pharmacy now for some tape to poultice the rabbit's leg? Neelam, please walk his personal note on behalf of the young Portuguese couple whose visas expired to the Magistrate's office and on the way back, pick up a packet of Ganesh beedies across the street. A British rocker with an acoustic guitar has just broken into Puri's favorite song, 'Wild World.' When Puri hears me in a corner meekly singing along, he steps directly in my face with a mission, challenging me to sing it loud – breaking into my 'Life' honed solitary – like I *should and can* lighten up now and sing along, no matter where I am coming from...and I do.

...   .

I see the same hologram of Puri's shadow on the black screen of my porch whenever the moon passes the trees behind. The tilt of his head and the hat that he wears can only mean one thing...and I read him clear, "Hell's Bells, Fisherman! Now is the time for Lovers to Love, Singers to Sing and Poets to Remember!"

I empty the shoebox onto my desk and turn up the light.

downtown Woodstock
1994

14

How I Spent My Summer Vacation

swift mystery jalaba'd men
eye-blink gone inside smoked corners –
spotted again half-hidden in portals magnetic
over-packed donkeys brass bell chime waddling up the hill
in The Casbah – droopy-eyed tapestry of a hundred still stares
disappearing into the staring motif always watching...
clank orchestra
to bazaar roar
minaret wail
thousand spices
donkey shit
strong coffee
blend in plumes
of genie breezes
swirling continuous
sensation camouflage
interrupted like a radio wave
that cuts out every 10 seconds –
in an instant
floating the entire canvas up
suspended in hush ether –
then quick slamming back down to
street of dreams
pressing every pore
up the hill, up the hill
in Old Tangiers –
for 5,000 years,
up the hill
to the Medina
and I will never go back,
never stop wandering up that hill
to the Medina.

Our Fearless Leaders

Buddha Say: You Must Try

Mohammed Say: You Must Not

Jesus Say: You Must Pay

Krishna Say: Beat The Check

My Generation

Lucky
To

Free

Love

Listen

Speak

Know

See

Each
Other

Our
Selves

The
Sky

Melt

The Sweet Second Called July

Putting And Seeing
My Garden
In Order Now
Brings Muscle Peace
Of Play

Like Being Stoned
Enough To
Remember
The Once
That Created
The Whole Feeling
Of 'Free'...

Certainly Day

        Lots Of It

Wear It Out
'Til It's Worn Out
Along With Yourself

Racing Raced
Thrill Thrilled
Moment In Breath
Of Moment Breath

Street-Run
Squeeze Every Ounce
Surface Skim-Ride Relentless
To Twilight Lonely Return –
Still Buzzed

        Everybody Home

        Bless Them

I Knew You When

I knew you when you
were old and young
at the same time
like an egg,
restless and dead,
ordinary and singular,
invested and abandoned

I knew you when you were
full, then emptied,
with nothing but Racism
to blame...

Old Newark, I knew you when
you broke
my heart
burning
under
my
wings

Veal Pizzaiola
(from Mama's Recipe Binder)

Ingredients:

a calf
canned plum tomatoes
garlic
dried oregano
capers
bay leaf
salt
pepper
white wine

--- --- ---

string up calf by hooves

skin

using strap
and buckle
whip leg until
it detaches from
the young animal

take a cast iron mallet
to separated meat until
it fragments,

with a butcher's knife
slice horizontally
into cutlets

choose a dozen and
beat them down again
until paper thin
and Rorschach-shaped,

set cutlets aside
on a frozen plate

stretch 12 canned plum tomatoes
on a chopping block until
the tops and bottoms snap off
and juices flow out –
discard juices

on a smaller chopping block
peal 4 cloves of garlic until
they glisten – snip gray parts

place cutlets on a clean platter
salt and pepper both sides

in a large fry pan, heat
3 tablespoons
blended oil

dreg cutlets in
well sifted flour,
soundly smacking
off excess

when oil is near boiling,
quickly sear cutlets
on both sides

remove and put aside cutlets
turn heat down

mince garlic,
toss in pan with
a heaped tablespoon of
baby capers,
lay in a bay leaf

rip tomato flesh
into length strips
toss into pan

shake and shake and shake
oregano stalks
over pan until leaves smatter

pinch in salt

simmer until tomatoes soften
(usually about 3 minutes)

put the cutlets back in
turn up the flame

find 3oz. of white wine
you can spare
add to pan

cook until you can't smell

remove from heat

picture yourself.

Kipke

blinded by my own blood
pinned on my back
legs curled high
like a fetus,
I swing wild up
from the edge of the gutter,
punching at my attacker's face
clamped tight between my knees –
while he strangles me
with a strong left hand,
banging a hammer around
my ear with his right

a sharp blow
whips one eye clear –
I see Benny Chaplo
handcuffed, rushing
Kipke with his
free fist –
with the other,
dragging a panicked Club 45
security guard
desperately trying
to unlock himself,
cop hat and glasses
flying
I know my brother
is out there...
6 on 3...
not good odds –
and it sounds
like War –
my head pressed
into the blacktop
of Bloomfield Avenue

... ...

twenty minutes before,
upstairs, Club 45...
me and Marty Romano
mesmerized by the first
Go-Go Girls
boogaloo watusi swim
slung above
either end of stage
in clear cube cages,
swish swishing
day-glo vinyl mini-skirts –
working bikini top bulge
through tip of
a *Happening* –
endless straight blonde hair
wild west coast swinging –
big blue eyes
dead ahead
into space –
hully-gully hitchhike heralding
a New Age hipdom –
Rhythm and Blues
serving up Soul
to must get stoned
white kids
at The Kearny Yacht Club
The Wagon Wheel
The Peppermint Lounge
The Green Door
The Paramount in Brooklyn
The Cotton Club in Newark
– Wildwood to Times Square –
tonight grooving
Rocky Rafanella's Club 45
– old North Ward –
Hippie Revolution
about to peek
long-haired Head
even into deep slick
silk mohair Newark –
hot Good Friday
1965

... ...

'Wooly Bully' fades boogie
Sam The Sham screeching
"Hey Dawg – Hey Dawg"
smothered in brass blast
Philly chain lead in
to 'The In Crowd' –
popping room up/Beat
with intimation of Summer –
Go-Go Girls Frug Jerking hard
breast thigh pounding iridescent
Liberation Drum...
pale...
steady...
almost visible...
on another track of the
psychedelic rollercoaster
tumbling the land of a
thousand wiseguys,
where your girl
JUST DOESN'T dance
with another guy!

'Shotgun' skips on
over Dobie Gray
still wailing
"...The In Crowd yeah yeah yay e-yuh" –
I catch Donna and Connie
dancing – and Donna's old boyfriend,
Kipke bopping across the floor to them
"Marty, I'm gonna bang that guy
over there"
"Go 'head Goots...I got your back" –
his eyes glazed
to the caged blondes...

robot of Pride
I march in
to battle
this big guy –
trouble if I win –

more trouble
if I lose –

"Don't fight – dance"
Connie
turns me in front of Donna –
in slide dance chance
that Kipke just backs off...
slide right
clap!
slam elbows back –
into Kipke's chest
slide left
clap!
slam elbows back –
into Kipke's arm
slide
clap!
slam elbows back
"WHAT THE FUCK
ARE YOU DOING?!"
he grabs my elbow
coming back –
spins me
to biggest fist
slow-motion
break my nose
split my eyelid
knock me out cold
One Punch

jolted half-awake
in darkness
press
of bodies on top
of me, I hear
Benny Chaplo,
my brother
and Skippy Frascatore
peeling hitters
off me

downstairs
Rocky Rafanella's boys
bring me to with smelling salts...
Kipke flies past
kicked out
with his crew
"I'll kill you, you motherfucker"
I yell –
five people
trying to keep me
from bleeding to death

one arm around Benny
my brother pushing
a towel into my gushing eye
we step out of Club 45
for Columbus Hospital...
Kipke smashes me
in the face,
flattening me –
his gang behind –
coming on again

        ... ...

"What are you gonna do about this Goots?"
"Kill that mother fucker
...as soon as I get this fuckin' patch
off my eye"

fuckin' patch on my eye
alibi mask
until I can heal
patch on my eye
shield against scorn
until I can heal

patch on my eye
my ticket out
of assault/retribution cycle...
my ass kicked too pitiful
to take any more

... ...

Thunderbird
Circling
Logorythmic
Hi-Tide Rennaissance Rush
Tripping
Military Park
downtown Newark,
I read aloud
'Starting From
San Francisco' –
mind already
split for Coast

across the park
I see Kipke
I still feel
the crush of his fist
my eye still stings
and aches...

Kipke – big as ever
he doesn't see me...
maybe I can beat
him over the head
with something...

Kipke, back a step
back a year
back a Life
that stalks me

"I hope you go to Vietnam
and Die Motherfucker!"
I hear myself whisper

... ...

a week later
on my way
out her door

for the last time,
I hear my mother
and Aunt Rose
over coffee
"...how terrible...
kid got killed
the day he landed
in Vietnam...
18 years old...
what a sin...
he was friends
with my Ralphie –
used to eat at
my house on Sunday...
big handsome Polish kid
Henry...
Henry Kipke
...what a sin

      ... ...

my secret –
inch and mile
of Shame –
toying with a Terror
chasing both of us

my jinx
a haunted footnote
attached
to a name
on a list of names
that would stretch
one by one
around the planet
before the killing was over –
The Hulking Reaper Vietnam
crashing the garden gate
of a generation
going
and gone

Once Upon a Time in 1967

"Get Out Here On The Flo!"
Jackie Wilson hop-skips
to the mic-stand,
swinging it to the side
like he's gonna kiss it –
as the room bops
with this slicked-back
Swami In The Promised Land –
his halo lighting the low, crescent
stage at the Whiskey a Go-Go
golden...

...and he's got all our Spirits
in the palm of his hand
and he's shakin' them like dice,
ready to roll –
sway snap shimmying
in three piece iridescent suit –
jacket soon slapped over his shoulder,
like a Gospel Sinatra strutting –
then tossed with vest up and behind
the drummer – as the show peels and pops,
'til he's down to white satin shirt
open to the waist –
Quaking, Wailing:
"Just Say You Wheel –
Say Hey You Whe-Heel!"

...his Quick Cha-Cha syncopation
getting between the beats
and our pulses
        ...then he closes
his big moon eyes and swoons us
in the eclipse – 'til he snaps back
smiling right into the gig...and
even the Go-Go Girls have stopped
to behold *this* man Workout!

'Cubby' – 11 year old
miniature Jackie Wilson,
right down to moves and shoes –
gets spot-lit to the stage –
and three numbers later –
Hot Fudge On Sundae –
Jackie flips Cubby
up onto his shoulders,
bobbing through the soul-struck
'Standing O' audience
and out pushed open fire-doors –
blending into a fuzz-boxed clamor
of the Whole World passing by...

              turning

      looking

                  Tripping

      on *Sunset Strip*,
    molting from Dino's Lounge
      to Diggers diaspora,
      Surf Music to Acid Rock,
      Boulevard to Mecca –
the swarming woven crowd,
drunk in Ultra-Hip,
unraveling The Great Mandala
like so much string
in Day-Glo length
of Concentricity
hanging out on this
hot Electric promenade
into light-air L.A. night –
contact psychedelicizing walk
– one side or the other –
of this laid out Ley Line
"Cool Cat"/"What It Is"/"Something Else"
West Village gone crazy on the Bus to
"!OH WOW!"/"Far Out"/"Freak"/
Purple Hazed first time for Everything
everything First Time

Happening...

– "Mr. Excitement," Jackie Wilson,
toting man-child ringer incarnation Cubby
piggy-back palanquined like Daddy's Baby Buddha –

last sighted
Lifting Higher And Higher
above the parade

Dickhead

#15
February 25

#15
by birth

#15
of Wiseguy Street

#15
just in from Hippie
barricade

#15
not made for
your Army
...and if you
try to take me today,
something really bad
is going to happen here

#15
herded
crew-cut Sergeant
to barking
crew-cut Sergeant

all around
every direction,
kids I played with
went to school with
hung-out with
on every
'Nicky Newark' corner
– all –
herded room to room
stripped down to underwear

no college deferment
no Probation deferment
no more
'deferment'
at all
available
for young men
of our Class –

only blind shuffle
luck of draw
Number...
innocent number...
Birthday number –
1 through 365
thrown into a hat
with future, dream
and memory –
shook-up with
20 billion other pieces
of a few million other lives –

all bets off
conversation over
all pretense abandoned
first picked
first delivered up
– to War –
– to Vietnam –
'Report For Duty'
date on the spot

The 'Lottery'
Draft Call
1970

#15
if they try
to take me now,
something very
bad is going to
happen here

behind
enemy lines
of seiging State

in a country declared
at war with itself
by its own government –
gone wild with Nixon
"Constructive Polarization"
Divide/Conquer
strategic purge
of all dissent:

White vs. Black
rich vs. poor
police/student
shorthair/longhair
parent/child –

Nixon's "Silent Majority" –
political cover for every
abuse of power

... ...

in cities:

'Search and Seizure' laws
suspended

bad cops recruited
and unleashed in
repression frenzy

F.B.I.
setting up
and busting
opposition leaders

C.I.A. smuggled
pure heroin
suddenly everywhere

dirt cheap –
dosing
The Psychedelic Revolution
to a halt –
defamed
in the
strung-out
dead
eyes
of its
should have been
next generation

on campuses:

right wing agents
swarm and agitate,
planted in 'Radical Left' masquerade:
– a building shut down –
– a computer blown up –
– a hostage taken –
media programmed
to play out like a Greek tragedy:
to the death

in households:

Father/Mother
 – brainwashed in
Fear Propaganda,
vote Law and Order
over son and daughter...

... ...

"When did you start using?"
(his head down scribbling)

I have passed every test –
eyes ears lungs and heart –
one more room
– The Psychiatrist –

and the entire shanghai
will no doubt be tied up tidy...
then I just don't
know what's gonna happen

"I don't use drugs"

he still hasn't looked at me

4 minutes silence

he rotates his face to me,
Woody Guthrie look-alike in uniform:

– "*I SAID*, when did you start using drugs?" –

I understand what he is doing
Seize the Moment
rattling off every drug I know

he huddles back over desk
scribbling fast for a minute –
hard stamping papers –

handing me one:

4F

        ... ...

sat out on gray stone Federal
building pile,
jumbled in
anger
calm
release
trauma,
looking for anyone else
who might have gotten
Lucky
and out...
I see 30,000 May Day

marching straight at me,
rah rah cheering/jeering
slogan/song,
pushing up/down/
forward/backwards
a 100 foot long penis –
Richard Nixon's head
for a tip –
full circus dressed
dancing clown
leading parade
landing next to me
with David Peele
"Up Against The Wall
Muthafucka" rasping
passing joints –

Object: to levitate
The Federal Building
12 feet in the air

*and just about that moment
…as the high priest clown pronounces
'mission accomplished!'
"It's floating!!!
The Whole Fucking building
is 12 feet in the air, Mannnn!
ha ha…SEE IT
it's 12 feet in the air Maannnn!"*

…and just about that moment
I spot the 'task force' agents
who put a 38 to my head,
planted joints on me
and threw me in jail
a year ago,
filming every face
in the writhing,
shrieking crowd

I spy the barking Sergeants
battle-facing down
from 10th floor windows –
unfazed

the goading clown
now juggles
painted grin bound

...*just about that moment*

I pass through the throng
out onto empty side streets

and *away* from America

Rumble Doll

you are not
my friend
        I am yours

to me,
what you do
is not as important
as what you do not do

my keys are yours
my blanket
my hand
my scent
my glance back
and my oath

my priests
and their toys
my heritage
my fight
the beauty of my face
the smile of the children

        The Leaf, The Pen,
        The Thunderbolt
        And The Ornament

take them all
along with Forever
back
with this dream
to the Temple Of Action

...which is part of the deal

I Saw You

I Know You Were There
I Saw You

Your Mother
Got Nasty With The Cops
Like She Always Did
And You Went Back
To The Basement
After The Fracas
And Continued Screwing
Beverly Davis –
The Finest Black Girl
In Grammar School –
Her Long Legs
Wrapped Around
Your Neck –
I Saw That Too
From The Side
Of The Doorway –
Wow! That Was
Something For A Kid
Like Me – Still Looking
For A Kiss!

The Day After
Me And Your Sister
Won 2nd Place
In The Twist Contest,
You Stepped In Dog Shit
With Your New Wingtips...
I Saw It And Called
You "Shitshoe" Loudly
In Our 7th Grade Class
You Had Just Been
Transferred To From
Reform School

You Banged Me
In The Face For That
And I Understood
That Our Best Friendship
Was Over

...And Now For
The Hard Part...
I Was There
On The Street
When Your Crippled
Stepfather Beat You
So Bad With His Cane
Out Onto The Stoop
Of Your Building
And You Ran Up
The Fire Escape
5 Stories
To The Roof
And Stayed There
At The Edge, Shivering
In Your Pajamas,
In A Big Blizzard.
Your Mother
Called The Cops
And They Got You Down
And Warned Your Stepfather.

When I Saw That,
I Knew That You
Were Worse-Off
Than Me And
Always Would Be

... ...

Over The Next
Dozen Or So Years
I Wrote 3 Poems
Wondering About
You In Jail
And Whether You
Were Out Yet:
One On A Canal
Barge In Amsterdam,
One From An Oasis
In The Sinai,
One From A Courtyard
In The City Of Thanjavur –
I Asked Myself
About The Luck
Of Freedom –
Why Me And Not You?
After All, You Were The
Brave One.

When I Returned
You Were On The
Front Page
Of The News
Along With Your
Brother And Sister –
Busted Kidnapping
The Richest Man
In America.

I Saw That
I Saw You

Now Everyone Did,
Even Me

Genard

Pete refused to come...
Vinny Biggs was in the hospital
getting part of his leg cut off
with Diabetes...
I dug up an old black silk suit
I remembered wearing to
Basin Street East, 8 years
and 'My Generation' before

too dark for a summer evening
too bright for a Funeral Home
too steep for a parking lot,
I trudge like a Sherpa –
looking like a priest
"man from the East"
just back from Tibet –
marking a path
across the boundaries
of our youth –
just down the block from
Bobby Fahrenger's house
and the last time I saw you...

                ... ...

"You wanna cop Goots?
I'm goin' to 17th Street
right now...you got $10?
We can get hi right now!

your neck chains strobing
in bright windshield sun,
as you lean across the front seat
popping the passenger door
of your 'Coupe de Ville'
to let me in
 – 'Cornudo' and crucifix
tangling unbuttoned,

bare chest reveal – framed in crisp,
pure white 'high-roll' shirt, tucked in
tailor-made charcoal gray, silk-mohair
pants with matching belt – Italian loafers
and short silk socks shining...
your hair perfect tight cropped waves –
no sideburns – face 'facial' clean – wicked
slim handsome as ever, looking me up and down twice
with wide eyes I understand:
"How the fuck could this have happened to one of us?"
– to *Goots*!?

shoulder-length hair, bare-chested under woven
Indian vest and 'Love Beads' – worn out bell-bottom
jeans held up with sash of drapery trim –
thick skin barefoot – big smile – 'Peace Sign.'

Your star-sapphire pinky ring flashes –
platinum wristwatch rolling, as we make
the turn from 18th Avenue on to Brookdale Avenue...

It's the 'Summer Of Love' – you picked
me up and gave me a lift out to South Orange Avenue,
near Celantano's, on the first leg of my California hitch...

"You wanna cop or not?" – mocking me again –
still picking a fight...

"When you gonna stop gettin' hi Genard?"

"When are *you* Goots?"
...as if were 1963...as if there were no difference
between Heroin and Psychedelics –
and we were still running partners

... ...

'The Three Musketeers and D'Artagnan':
Pete, me, Vinny Biggs and you – D'Artagnan –
behind 'The Projects' on Munn Avenue
looking for kicks in a Big City up and around us
we ran corner to corner
Invincible

Pete's sister Rosemarie introduced me to Patty
We sat on her big porch after school
and I thought I really had a chance
with this Beehive Bardot Angel
who seemed to like me –
then, you two showed up
at Sacred Heart Church one Sunday
in the first row balcony...
I watched you both touching and giggling
and knew that she loved you...
and why not? You were the 'best looking'...
she was the 'best looking'...
I never really had a chance.
So I learned how to see her as a cousin –
and to worry – because I knew you
and I knew that someday
you would break her heart bad.

           ... ...

Your father Michael stopped pacing
when he saw me walking toward
your coffin. He shook my hand hard
like a lifeline – wet with fear and grief
for his only son he knew once
had had 'words' with me in a time
his eyes grasped for.

I saw you, pasty-pale and laid-out –
still slick...still with that almost smirk...
still chiseled, handsome, bad D'Artagnan...
still the same wise-ass I knew...

she spoke my name as clear and loud
as she could, crushed in fits of sob and cry.
she saw my face as I saw hers – Perfect
in teenage trance – separated by teenage whim,
as I bent to kiss her for the first and last time,
her tear burst on my lips – a tear for us
and who we might have been – a tear for
you and how it happened –
a tear for the rest of her
young life, now shrouded.

I walked out solo like I came in,
past seats of the big crowd
from everywhere –
the docks, with respect for your father –
all the Fantasias
and all the families
with respect for them –
respect for a time and a bond and a duty,
in a place where what happened to you
just did not happen – stabbed 11 times
and left for dead
in a Harlem 'shooting gallery' vestibule
by strangers.

In the parking lot
the girls – gathered around cars,
cigarette smoke and now 'Disco' glitter –
call my name, like
I am some kind of hero
just for landing back
in the neighborhood

Patty's tear branded
on my lips...
thinking about
the time I sent 12 large pizzas
to your house on a Tuesday night
and let you blame it on
Sally Beans...

thinking about the day you showed-up
sitting diagonally behind me
in Sophomore English, just
transferred from Catholic school
and your loud mocking laugh, goofing
on me for twisting my Confirmation ring
around on my finger like I always did –
goofing on me –
like that was O.K. for a 'new guy' to do...

you always said that someday
we would 'come to hands'...
we never did
we never will
we should have
while we had the chance...
just to get even
just to get over
just to get right

alone inside my old suit
alone with your murdered Soul
alone with the 100,000 miles in between
I hear the girls still buzzing behind –

> *seeing the high plateaus and*
> *valleys climbing up from Pathankot*
> *to Dharamsala*
> *to Gamru-Tika*
> *and the mighty rim of the Himalayas –*

stationed at the core
of dissonance,
passing Bobby Fahrenger's house,
hanging a left
straight down
18th Avenue.

Provincetown
(to Pete)

_____

I went back and saw the place
you abandoned me with goodbye
the night of The Kent State
Massacre...as if you had had a
premonition that the 'Hippie
Movement' had become too
dangerous...and that scared
you enough to admit to yourself
that I would have to be left
alone with my head
from here on

I went back to the room
the world tilted with
its own trouble –
the one where your face
went from flesh to cement
and in one glance,
shunned our youth together –
taken away from sense and feeling –
forced to surrender our laughs,
release the safety of our bond
and suffer the things
that only we two know

I went back to the fireplace
we huddled, guests of
our saviors, at the end
of this end road rambled
through blind fog
as fast as Angels would fly –
disillusion to defiance –
Peace Love and everybody's business
to nobody's –
South Orange Avenue
to Commercial Street
solid non-stop –
just like always –

Proud from alley/rooftop/corner/
schoolyard/hustle/
'Nicky Newark'/wiseguy rule/
Village Beat Cool/
Acid/Barefoot/Brave
Longhaul Groovin'
Best Friend Legend
'Pete & RePete'
Coast to Coast
Solid

I went back to this
wilded place –
traced of dream
and faith –
curled with time
and your death
to redeem a moment –
our last –
crashing a fate frozen
overexposed
the day before yesterday –
brought with many, many
more miles –
along longshore dock
for you –
gone at horizon walk
for me

Blood Brothers lit out
from Pilgrim's first land
ever

Grandma Starshine's Long Simmering Stew

Ingredients:

1½ cups chopped onion
¼ cup minced garlic
8 oz. tofu cubed
1 cup peeled & cubed potatoes
1 cup carrots cut in cubes
1 28oz. can plum tomatoes
drained and rough chopped
½ cup frozen peas
4 oz. dry white wine
2 tsp. Herbes de Provence
3 tbsp. sunflower oil
½ tsp. salt
fresh ground pepper to taste

Preparation:

heat oil in large,
warm soup pot

add garlic controlling
heat so it doesn't burn
as you add Tofu
and lightly brown
on all sides

add white wine and reduce by half

stir in carrots, potatoes and tomatoes,

cover and cook for 15 minutes

uncover, add peas,
Herbes de Provence,
salt and pepper.

simmer uncovered for 10 minutes.

... ...

Starshine, pregnant big-time
fell off her bicycle
and broke her ankle
in front of the Deli
me and Pete happened
to be outside of
in Provincetown

we carried her, arms
around shoulders,
home to Rick,
breaking Action Paint
unchaining himself
showing us to the yard
on his way out to hospital
with Starshine

casted and crutched,
she sits in kitchen
walking me (her stand in)
Executive Chef style,
herb to heat with the vegetables
I had picked in her garden
by the beach,
a few days after They invaded
Cambodia

... ...

Fireplace winding down,
long day wrapped
well into night...The Artist, The Chef
and their baby asleep upstairs...us
on the couch, fresh from The Front...

Hippies Very Hip Pocket
Psychedelic Freewheeled
Through the 60's,
we are here...
in quiet End

...alone...
away from our town
away from our tribes
away from the music...
I turn on the T.V. for distraction...

May 4th, 1970
The Kent State Massacre

... ...

Thirty or forty million faithful – talking Thomas Paine – thinking

Constitution – countrymen and women – battered by the State.

You might expect people of all ages and stripes to rise and smash

the palaces of power. That's how this country got started. But in

this America, a gimmick has been perfected by the Nixon

Regime: 'Constructive Polarization' – revealing a stark bigotry at

the center of material comfort and a gap bigger than culture

between generations – programmed to play like Greek Tragedy:

to the death.

Exposed by their own offspring as caring more for security than

truth; possessions than freedom – protection than integrity –

debased and humiliated to their core, parents feed themselves to

a Monster created by the government they voted for in Hippie

fright hysteria – a Monster stifling all dissent and with every

breath, defending racism and injustice in the guise of 'law and

order.'

This Monster is impersonal and recognizes no allegiance to anything but the cult of repression that is its hoary flesh. Not happy with just politics, businesses, churches and schools, the Monster has now sprung through a window left open – into the households of America and with its steeled hook claws is ripping apart families like they never existed...like no one knows each other and the only thing important is which side you are on – 'Constructive Polarization' reaching its ultimate: Father against Son...Mother against Daughter...and when the shots ring out at Kent State and no one raises a hand and no one says, "Hey, Stop!... and when those who fought around the world for the future of their children, watch them lying wounded and dying right in front of them on T.V., it's like: 'they got what they deserve' and the official explanation is a lie and they let it pass with some kind of 'benign neglect' like it doesn't matter and no one can be organized to do anything but whimper...

and when those bodies

are lowered into the ground,

anonymous,

already forgotten –

Compassion silenced

by the bayonet of mass fear

and the heavy, burning fog of mass deception –

they take The Movement with them

...   all faith

and hope...

as the Bold moment

of "Peace and Love"

is concluded

with the demon Monster

roaring from his den...

where he hides today

In Plain Sight

Empire

"Hey John Wayne!
Get Yo Muthafuckin'
Feet Off Mah Heed!!
...Fuck You Want,
The Whole
Muthafuckin' Bench?"

I am stretched out
claiming the only
good spot,
pulling my blood-stiff
overcoat tight like skin
over my hospital gown –
most of my brow
mangled in gashes
bandaged tight

people tucked underneath
people pressed against each other
covering the floor
to toilet partition
Puerto Rican kid perches
swinging like monkey
in tree, tugging cell bars
bitching that his "Deal
woulda gone down
just about now –
...fucked-up
by little shitty Possession bust
by dumb-fuck cop" –
10th this year –
swears he'll be out,
week, ten days tops

Hindu guy
who fought a pack
when they insulted his wife –

sits straight like Ganesh –
black blood-blushed eye
busted nose
tangerine-sized lump on head –
will lose job and apartment
if he is not out
by Monday

everyone else is Black
20 of us in 15'x 20' cell
jammed tense

"Hey John Wayne!"
big face Black guy
peeks up again like Godzilla –
stone killer drenched eyes bulging,
quarter inch wide
never stitched scar
from bottom of one ear
right down to the corner
of albino-spotted
balloon lips –
cold-blooded
nothin' to lose gape
nudges me

"Maybe you wanna switch places
John Wayne, so I can stretch out
a little bit"

everyone gets very quiet

"I'm fine just where I am"

Scarface Godzilla goes still
for long second
clicks neck
blasts a roar like a laugh
up to monkey Puerto Rican

"Muthafuckin' John Wayne
is Muthafuckin' fine
right where he Muthafuckin' is!"

Puerto Rican kid smiles down
confirming that no one –
not even Scarface Godzilla
is going to fuck with me

short fat sister guard
like mail pushes curling
hard edge American bread
waxed bagged sandwiches
through bars

sat up like slaves in galley
breaking drumbeat row
– it's time to eat –
and all I see is my
China Doll Marilyn
in the Emergency Room
cut up – Beauty ruined –
as cops raise me up
from unconsciousness
fit me into my
blood soaked overcoat
ratchet on handcuffs
and drag me away
– numb with capture –
wondering what the fuck happened
outside the Empire Diner

... ...

Ringside Potala Of Momentum
Hard Blue Milled Gizmo Nexus
– fanned taut with evacuation
in annual Passover respite –

fractal red-green
'Tis the Season neon gleam –
occasional winking
lingering shadow of ritual frenzy –
shrouding National Holiday wake

storefront space darkened with
contortion of this single 'time out'

avenues cleared of business roll
strung traffic lights creaking
in silent night

...not even a Deli open

NYC – late Christmas night

1989

...nowhere to be caught
sticking out and hungry

... ...

play model London
Gramercy Park Hotel
eerie Hitchcock set
waiting for the murder
looks open

– same old revolving door
sharp right to
dim lounge
Goldfish cracker/moldy carpet stench –
tonight not even pianoed
by always far off key
silver gray pompadoured crooner

"Sorry...kitchen closed early –
half hour ago at 10"
back-up bartender regards
our desperation

stranger who hasn't said 5 words
in 12 years
lone customer holding up
the long/always airless bar
appears before us

eyes dilating
big teeth smile
snifter in hand

"...drinks are on me!
and what will you two
lovebirds have!?"

3 way over-pour Hennessey's
and Stoli's later –
now looped back to car
headed for last resort
24/7
Empire Diner

            ... ...

too bright
counter vacant

bowl of Chili/Heineken
Turkey Sandwich/Stoli
        world is our oyster

but when do we eat?

30 minutes later
nothing but
Heineken/Stoli

"Fuck this place!
Let's get in the car,"

drunker hungrier angrier

Marilyn yells from passenger window
suddenly attentive waiter
screams out to sidewalk behind me
hand slaps hard my shoulder
spins me
jumps me
swings at my face

I swing back
hustle into car
another waiter
banging my window –
I floor it the same second
another waiter appears
smack in front of car
waving arms wild –

I see him slow roll across hood –
he can't be hurt – rolled too slow –
I pull out quick
ripping for home

click right
crack right
from the left
BOOM!

... ...

"Where am I?"

"Saint Vincent's Hospital"
young good looking Italian cop
at bedside looks down
with paisano eyes

maybe somebody tried
to hurt me
and he is here to help

"Can I go home now?"

"Home? You're going to jail"

handcuff slap
just as nurse pulls
back drape
I see Marilyn
in bed across
blood red line
from crown to nose

      ... ...

eyewitness
Sergeant Santoro
fills in gaps
from front seat
of Squad Car
off for 'The Tombs'

I beat the check
knocked out one waiter
slammed into car
parked behind me
ran over another waiter
sped through red light
on Tenth Avenue
leaving the scene
hit 2 parked cars
on 23rd Street
swerved across
oncoming traffic
then crashed into a tree
smashing Marilyn and my foreheads
through the windshield
of the accordioned
Honda they
cut us out of

      ... ...

"Damn John Wayne...
looks like you caught
the Muthafuckin' jackpot
this time out"

'the jackpot'

Godzilla shakes his big head down

we trade sandwiches
olive loaf for American cheese

Papaya Delight

Ingredients:

1 ripe Papaya

12oz. fresh
goat's milk curd

plump raisins

fresh picked
large tropical flowers

fresh picked neem leaves

--- ---

moments before dawn's crack explodes
between peaks behind –
while your teacher sleeps –

slip out of hemp-strung bed
to kitchen across main room
of whitewashed, slate shingled,
cow dung, hay and earth brick
farmhouse $6 monthly rented...
fetch metal container...

hush out the door
to stone path winding
mountain jungle Himalayan rim
down to K.B. Dharamsala

pick 2 neem leaves
from tree,
begin chewing over
rope-bridged ravine

when teeth, gums and mouth
squeak clean and
village is clear in sight through mist,
(about 10 minutes)
spit out neem leaves

head direct to
goat's milk shop
where proprietor
long ladles just risen
curds into your container.
smiling behind slow boiling pan
the width of his lotused legs

pick best papaya at last market
back up the mountain as daybreak chill
begins to burn off and fruit sweats

cross bridge again returning,
pick large flowers of colors unnamed,
being careful not to strip
petal framed, leaf tapestried
miniature sightings of distant
Kangra Valley far below

rewind mountain to
your door, all quiet of
anything.

sink long stems into vase
on look-through to teacher's
slumber turning

on flat stone in cool kitchen,
slice papaya in half lengthwise

with pads of middle fingers
wipe black pearl seeds from
each papaya, being careful not to scrape
silken pocket they lay in

place papaya halves skin side down
on flat plank

heap goat's milk curd
into each pocket until
full and mounded

pepper mounds with
a few plump raisins

set aside

join awakened teacher in main room
hands clasped in first position

breathe, move
stretch loose looser in one hour
Yoga floor dance she has taught
through Spring

Finish

Breathe

sit growing at floor-length
Tibetan braids she untwines
for a hundred long brushes
until Scandinavian Goddess
vision in front of you –
head to toe
in sunburst of Blonde,
shrouding Cavaillon
breasts,
sky eyes
blue sparkling bullets
piercing all anticipation
now gone wild
with albino birthmark
between her legs,
gently clouding
from button of her belly –
set off with a shock of
blazing bright red pussy hair

pick her up
lay her down on soft wool blanket
over straw mat floor

screw until you
feel your butt flying
(about 15 minutes)

come like a forsaken dragon

she remains unimpressed

plate papaya

Serve.

Becoming

as soon
as all this
snow melts
Buddha is gonna
crack in half

– then his eyes will
wink at each other,
Lotus busted,
butternut belly split pear,
knees spread up from mud,
grin turned crescents,
Nothingness exposed,
mortar flesh to sky –

at that point,
I'll have to see
if they still carry them
at the Boiceville Nursery

A Thousand Steeples Deep
(to Leonard Cohen)

when no one was alone
you gave Loneliness
when Peace meant Love
you just stared –
'be here now' – left to
rooms of rooms
flames of flames
holy of holy
sin of sin

blood-heart
of Human human
phoning in
cruelty of dirt earth/
rapture of dirt earth –
until we cannot speak

then you depart dearly
...and when we bang
for even more:

Chorus sings chorus upon chorus
hallelujah heard upon hallelujah

Hallelujah

two-timing muesli

Ingredients:

3 cups rolled oats
¾ cup rye flakes
¼ cup chopped pistachio nuts
¼ cup chopped hazelnuts
¼ cup pumpkin seeds
½ cup chopped Medjoul dates
½ cup dried apples
½ tsp. cinnamon
½ tsp. vanilla
3 oz. coconut oil
2 tsp. brown sugar
½ tsp salt

Preparation:

– preheat oven to 350 degrees
– mix oats, nuts, seeds, cinnamon, dried apples and salt
– mix in coconut oil, vanilla and brown sugar
– bake at 350 degrees for 20 minutes on parchment
  covered baking sheet
– remove from oven and mix in dates
– return to oven for 5 minutes
– remove from oven and let set on stovetop

... ...

– looking straight ahead
without a blink, you throw
your hat over my just
rock-hard cock,
our bus turning into
Old Jerusalem first sight –

then you put your hand under
your hat and squeeze
all the way down to Lion's Gate
without a blink
because you Want me

like I Wanted you
at dawn Kibbutz Sasa
up a ladder picking first apple
of the day that is always eaten

exposing in its place
your Botticelli Angel face
on the other side
up a ladder
with first apple –
blue Kibbutzim capped
as if you weren't
Romansh Swiss
and Mystic Nephrodite
to boot

　　　　… … …

"Hashish! Opium! Heroin!"
The dealer whispers loud

again, as we pass,
Hashish! Opium! Heroin!

you don't notice him
I shoot him an Old Newark look –
we pass by

I hear from behind:
FUCK YOU!
FUCK YOU AND YOUR COUNTRY!
then
FUCK YOU AND EVERYONE YOU KNOW!
then
FUCK YOU AND YOUR MOTHER!

I look back and
see him flash a switchblade

YOU DON'T BELIEVE ME!!
I'LL CUT YOUR FUCKING EARS OFF!
he comes running
waving blade

in my pocket
I open six inch
Hunter's knife
I picked up in Nazareth

without a whisper
to Elsbeth
I know I can stop this guy
– if I have to –

except I want to
make love to her
in the next few minutes
more than I want to
stab a mad at America
mad drug dealer...

rushing her
dashing through
Lion's Gate
and into the
best bed
of the first hotel
we see,
I truly learn
the value
of making a run for it

... ...

at home on Kibbutz,
trekking Sasa to
top of Mount Merom
watching waves break

30 miles away near Nahariya,
blue cedar Lebanon
over the hill in front of us,
we vow marriage/Mexican beach/
me novel/you nurse

nothing surer.

you back to Bern
good hospital gig tomorrow
me South to Eilat for
ticket money to meet
you there
– your Haifa Poste Restante
letter by Christmas Eve
to confirm –

in Commune kitchen
we bake muesli
on the farm
in the hills
on the border
where Love found us
and follows us
Witness

... ...

5 a.m. 105 in shade slave
short-short Pyramid payback
Eilat desert construction
for only Goy
lire allowed in Holy Land:
$12 every day –
all sinew, sun and muscle
lean of sexual relief and amongst
the international same –
burnt hands then bled to landscape
she-she Israeli Nouveau Yuppie gardens –
later – old Palestinian restaurant pot scour to
spotless ready for tomorrow's lamb

– saving for Christmas Eve –
Post Restante
Haifa
Bern
Elsbeth

... ...

'til Anot shows up
drop dead honey-baked
Marilyn brunette
Sabra rasp swoon
sweet flesh lick
Sinai Taba beach
laid in eclipse
– exodus to her 1st wadi outside Eilat
'House of Tea & Flowers' hot spot –

business booming enough to live,
screw by day and every night
roof pulled back to
full stud stars
– Simple –
simply making tea, music,
cookies and Peace
in Yom Kippur
'Wild West' War zone
between deserts
and histories...

Christmas Eve,
Haifa
and Elsbeth
come and gone

... ...

'til I get back from
Negev Tin Mine toil
to find long beard boxer short
Barry from Vancouver
in same Anot bed
– roof pulled back –

... ...

Race to Haifa Poste Restante!
(no letter there)
Race Fate!
Race hard Europa winter hitch North!

Race to Elsbeth's door open!

to behold her
and her psychologist
fiancée 'Kurty' –
his head turned
to me,
wide smiling,
strong with Love's
serene promise –
bent over open oven

baking muesli

Summer Coq au Vin

Ingredients:

Chicken
Wine
Olives
Cognac

... ...

Decant recommended
Saumur Champigny rouge
set aside

find a proper
Sancerre

roam yard sipping it
at every glance –
stone bench, to patio chair,
to rocker, to lawn, until
bottle is empty and on its side
under hammock.

see what is happening
back in the house

have a few olives

recline in sunroom
with Saumur Champigny.

rail at evening news
with jaws clenched,
banging remote like
Clark Gable firing
torpedoes in
'Run Silent,
Run Deep'

have some olives

return to hammock
with remainder of
Saumur for 'research
and development'

bring empty decanter
to kitchen,
have some olives
while fumbling for menus.

– Buddha's Table
679-1334

Choose any item, numbers
34 thru 46 (best to avoid
the labor complicated
'Moo Shu Chicken')

or

– Angelina's
679-5392

Chicken Parmigiana
Sandwich

or

– Jicama Juan
679-2178

Chicken Cheese Enchiladas

Pop and Slurp
Big Sloppy Malbec
to pair

scoff delivery immediately
upon arrival
(preferably
in private).

retire to hammock
full stomach,
Van Morrison on
portable CD,
backscratcher armed
– cognac to taste –
– twilight to star bright –

(careful not to flambé!)

Cold Sweat

*"The man got his **dick** cut off!! You still think I'm jivin' you, Pete? My cousin Earl was a 'Famous Flame' and he does not lie! Check any picture of James Brown before 1965...check out between his legs...an' look at him now! He went to England and got himself made into a woman..."*

*Greg has snuck me up past the old elevator guard I saw 5 days a week, every week, before I dropped out – up to the roof where we used to smoke joints at lunch hour. There won't be any lunch hour or joints today...it's 9:30 a.m. ...we've come up to see what's happening and walk toward our old perches, each leaning on one of the twenty foot high letters "PUBLIC SERVICE ELECTRIC & GAS CO." that loom over downtown and all the neighborhoods straight up to the low rolling South Orange Mountains on the horizon. At about this point, Greg would be repeating his schtick about James Brown's supposed sex change operation, where he insists that I study the crack between James Brown's legs where his penis used to be. Greg would get into it, then I would commence my all-excited-and-serious-like routine, insisting that he and his cousin Earl were both out of their minds and how it is impossible to change a man into a woman. Then Greg would just look at me and sly smile with his stick mustache and cool-tint David Ruffin style glasses wedging up, giggling through his spaced front teeth, because he had gotten me going again and that goof was enough to get us into each other's heads and humor on a safe bridge between our two different worlds; our two different countries — his **Black** America – mine **White** America — just a few blocks and a fire wall of hate away from each other, there in summer July Newark on the first day of the Riot of 1967.*

*How many times on that roof had I let down my guard and
trusted Greg – the first Black person I ever smoked with? How
many times had he blown my mind with a quick question – or a
look – or a nod, as I paraded the litany of ignorance and hatred I
had been brought up with – almost confessing them – before
healing eyes? Why did Black girls start screwing way before
White girls? Aren't Blacks "out to get" Whites? If Blacks aren't
inferior, then why do they look like apes? Isn't Martin Luther
King part of a Communist plot to take over America? With each
prejudice exposed we were binding something special between
us...liberating something about equality... ...about brotherhood.*

*When Greg asks me to baptize his first son, flying in the face of
his recently converted Black Muslim brothers, I accept, without
thinking twice about the world around us. But that world is about
to separate us, and this time, not even James Brown's sex
change could have broken the ice as we step to the end of that
roof.*

... ...

We weren't supposed to be friends. It was against every rule of
our domains. In his, the Central Ward, White people were
Devils, Crackers and White Trash. In mine, the West Ward,
Black people were Niggers, Mulanyans and Tootsoons, never
allowed to set foot over the line. In 1961, down the block from
my grammar school, I saw a Black man who had walked into
our neighborhood, tied by rope to the back of a car and keel-
haul dragged down cobblestone 15th Avenue until he
disappeared. When the guys came back to the corner, they
laughed loud and told us that the nigger was dropped back
where he 'belonged' – a few *miles* down – past Hunterdon
Avenue – they didn't know if he was dead or not and they didn't
care at all. A matter-of-fact, unwritten law said that you could
do stuff like that and it was O.K. ...even *good*. No hesitation...
No guilt...No fear...in plain sight.

In the early 60's, Black migration from the South pushed the
color line up into our streets and the neighborhood started to
'change' – whites move out fast, mostly to all-white Vailsburg...
not before taking one last kick and swing at the intruders.
From ten and twelve year old swastika-badged gangs whipping

across a playground, hands locked in a long chain, trampling any black kid in their path, to schools where teachers turned away, refusing to deal with the issue, as acquiescence became the only curriculum – to the streets once said to be "paved with gold" when my father arrived from small town Sicily – streets now abandoned as if no one had ever lived on them, their history stripped away in disgrace – the black migration was an invasion of hungry, dangerous lepers who had taken over our homes and forced us out running.

The riots began in 1964 with federally forced "bussing." Black kids were pushed into Vailsburg High, where out of control young wiseguys made the rules and their turf of brutality, gambling, extortion, larceny and gang bangs thrived undisturbed by a hint of discipline from cowardly teachers and administrators afraid for their own safety. Every single day black kids were jumped in the halls, jumped in the playground, jumped in the lavatories, jumped in the gym, jumped in the classrooms and jumped on the buses until they refused to be bussed. By the time that summer came, the scene was set for big trouble when the Feds decided that the public pool on Boylan Street should be integrated. Whites went crazy. Any Blacks who made it from the bus stop to the locker room were attacked by a waiting crowd and forced out. More Blacks came, this time with Police escort, past the locker room and into the water, only to face a line of a few hundred white kids stretching right across the pool, splashing as they advanced, screaming "2, 4, 6, 8 WE DON'T WANT TO INTEGRATE!" – cornering the blacks till they gave up and left with their half-hearted guards following. Within a week, violence escalated into a full-scale White riot out on South Orange Avenue where the Blacks waited for the bus back to from where they came.

I ran those streets that day next to Crazy Billy Ferranto, a bat-wielding, thirty-year-old maniac. I kept my mouth shut, hoping it would all end before someone got killed. I would just get through another big fight and try not to get hit, then everyone would disappear into cars and down side streets as usual. But this one was going on too long and too wild...like we didn't even have to worry about cops. Crazy Billy speeded up, hollering, "Come on, let's get dees niggers!"

I saw George Higgenbotham with his sister and younger brother, cowering in the doorway of Sis's Candy Store. George and his family were the only blacks living in Vailsburg at that time. Everyone knew them and liked them, including Crazy Billy who lived on the same block. I greeted George in my usual, friendly way as if he were safe – my usual friendly way... *like we were in cafeteria study period laughing at me flicking spitballs all over a sadistic teacher's back each time he passed my desk looking for a reason to stick me with central detention... or waving to George and his sisters, hot summer sequestered all out on his porch like our audience on Munn Avenue, as we marched out to the corner every night to take our places dressed sharp as a tack...or streaking back past them the other way running from the cops...or on a few Sundays in the Fall every year for the ritual neighborhood against neighborhood tackle football games, organized by wiseguys as if they were 'sports' and never getting past half time without a gang fight if we were losing, in Vailsburg Park where George was the quarterback no matter what color he was 'cause nobody could run or throw the ball like him...*George looked back at me with panic in his eyes and before I had a chance to blink or think, Crazy Billy beat George and his sister hard over the head with his bat, then threw it through the store window at them as they ran inside for shelter, both of their faces covered with blood. Later, behind the Raydan diner, Crazy Billy stuck an old car muffler into a twelve-year-old Black kid's chest. He was congratulated garrulously, as all the young wiseguys took up their stations in the back booths of the diner.

Over the next few years, the boundaries between White and Black neighborhoods hardened. Blacks did not step into Vailsburg and it became dangerous for a White to head down below the Parkway overpass, where a loud and angry militancy was rising. Across town in the North Ward, Anthony Imperiale was instructing his storm-trooper vigilantes in martial arts, police strategies and the articles of White Supremacy, as his armed patrols sealed Blacks in their ghetto. Ignorance upon Fear, atrocity upon atrocity, the City of Newark, founded 200 years before the Civil War, was configuring for self-destruction.

*From the roof we stood stiff staring out on the "civil disturbance"
turning Occupation and it felt like a chill suddenly sliced between
us, careening pieces of what we were and what we had become
together over the edge, smashing to the erupting streets below –
our trust in the future – any shelter at all...tumbling out and over,
leaving only heartache, our friendship smothered, our soul rap
laughter buried in an avalanche of hurt crashing down. We were
each watching chunks of our lives blow up descending;
memories, in a town of memory, tossed over – burning –
exploding...*

*Just below, columns of Army tanks, troop trucks and armored
vehicles with machine guns mounted, roll across Broad Street
toward the South Ward where fire and shots crackle in waves.
To the right in the Newark Street section past Military Park,
something just blew-up big – bursts of gunfire now ringing.
Further up, all around the Central Ward, more fires in Greg's
neighborhood – long legged machine guns perched on rooftops.*

*On Fourteenth Avenue in the West
Ward – flames rise high, as houses and blocks go up — houses
with my memories soaked into walls — blocks of histories laid in
like bricks where my father sunk his feet in and met my mother,
where all the people we knew, each with his own family around;
each coming from their own village or city somewhere in Italy,
were attached to everyone else in New World aspirations and Old
World custom, in this "Mannaggia l'America!" outrageous place
they had arrived to work, to escape, or to hustle – this fast place
that people from every part of Europe called theirs – each with
their own section – Italians and Irish in the West Ward, Italians in
The North Ward, Italians and Spanish 'Down Neck,' Jews,
Germans and Slavs in the East Ward, Polish and more Italians in
the South Ward...Guineas, Micks, Spics, Kikes, Krauts and
Polacks...all bonding, with the assurance of family to their
struggles – trying to make sense in a country that welcomed them
in, then called them names.*

Littleton Avenue burning to the ground...Littleton Avenue, where our greenhorn families gathered every Sunday, happy to be overfed and together...

*except one Sunday, on my fourth birthday, everyone is cursing ugly talking about moving. We **had** to move quick. 'Niggers' moved in next door and I sneak out to the backyard to get away and a kid across a brand new Cyclone fence four times our height, is my same age, staring at me just like I am staring at him – friendly – curious – a little hurt in both of our eyes...maybe a little more in his... and I start to wonder what is going on.*

"Hey, you know something?"
"No."
"...You're a nigger."
"What's a nigger?"
"Somebody who's black."
"I'm not black...I'm brown."
...and he is right
...and I see that 'Black' is not about color.

...Littleton Avenue, where my Grandfather made wine in his cellar and became the local street sweeper when he was put out of a construction job after a wheelbarrow full of bricks fell on his face and spread his nose ear to ear and his oldest son, my father, became the breadwinner for a family of six.

Fire straight down Fairmount Avenue. When I was eleven I hung out past midnight at Apple's Pool Hall there with the old guys and learned how to shoot pool and gamble – around the block from 14th Avenue – where we marched in The Feast from my church to my grammar school, now studded with flames —

...more on Ninth Street, where my best friend, Jerome, his kid brother and his sister, Frances, my first girlfriend, had lived...

to Eighth Street, to Seventh Street —
from Springfield Avenue,
where my mother waitressed
for twenty-five years —

down every alley of my childhood,
I see the places of my past
disappear in the thin summer sky

State troopers and Newark Police are all over town, surrounding every housing project with two hundred gun stakeouts, waiting for a pin to drop before firing into every window, killing innocent women and children in their trigger panic. As we watch, a hundred sirens and dozens of fire trucks scream speeding through the smoke. All businesses are about to close and the streets to be cleared by a total curfew at the tip of a Riot that would last for five days, killing many more Blacks than reported and dooming Newark to Federal takeover.

*I don't remember what we said as the command to evacuate blared up from loudspeaker trucks, but I never forget the dead, mute anger in Greg's eyes, I searched for connection at that moment – our last moment together – before he quickly sinks his head surrendering...surrendering Hope, for he **has** to take a militant side now, in the face of this slaughter...and because I am White, I am on the other side. We turn from the roof and split – more distant from each other than when we first met.*

there, in that fire,

I say so long to a city

sucker punched

by its own sick soul...

stunned...

twisting...

out on its feet

and about to drop...

and there too, I leave Greg,

whose life bonded me

to a truth

that still cries out.

Poet's Chair
(for Swami Tommy)

I saw a movie again
with your name listed
as Writer/Producer
and I Googled,
just to see if it was
really you

...then I saw 'PittBrad'
among your 'League
of Poets' "friends"...
and then you, with
Pre-Hippie goatee –
just like Newark, 1965 –
when a few wiseguys
up and went Beatnik

you showed up
in my world
reciting poetry on the street
at the crossroads
of our country –
the crossroads
of our lives –
on downtown campus,
1968

I right away admired
your Brains...your Cool...
...your Style...and did
again much later at
'Freedom' commune Upstate...
and in the West Village,
even more later

...and do once again
in my imagination –
you carrying Old Newark Grail
to Brangelina –

with Brains, Cool and Style

you made 'Big Movies'
about who we are and
where we're from – 'Big Stars'
playing our parts...
last year on 'The Information
Highway' we clicked again...

fantastic and inspiring,
you had moved your
Hollywood office
much closer to
'who we are and
where we're from' –
to the Cathedral –
setting up shop under
the remains of an old
fishing pier – half washed
away by 'Superstorm Sandy' –
its ruins bannered by the anthem
'Down The Shore
Everything's Alright'
on a salvaged piece of itself
atop last piles standing
out to sea.

I met you there –
your calls coming in
from Germany, Hollywood,
China – you, seeped in your
white, canvas Producer's chair –
as if 'The System' bends
to you...
I was impressed, pitching
my particular Mob Drama drama
layed out on the sand

... ...

I have returned with another Summer
like we always did – to that beach –
but now with curious heart, to see
if you might still be there – an
echo of who we were – Prince/Kings
harmonizing under that boardwalk –
out of the sun – washing our Spirit clean –
heavened by 'The Shore'

if I had seen you more than once
in 40 years, I might not have repeatedly
embarrassed my ocean soaked soul – getting
right in the face of anyone passing
that even slightly reminded me of you,
walking the swirling tide's edge
to and from that pier, like always, drying off –
returned, now tugged by the chance that
maybe – just maybe –
I have a running partner
still alive and kicking –

to find your chair in place

– empty –

1,2,3,...4 days –
in place
empty

'til last night
Blood Moon Rise
Over Beach Of Our Blood

      empty again to my witness
      under that boardwalk
      listening for the
      happy sound of a carousel
      just almost
      not quite
      alone

Untitled

Poetry is
Rapid Transit
for the Soul

IT WHISPERS
IN THE DELUGE

WHISPERS
IN THE SUNLIGHT...

WHISPERS
IN THE MIDST
OF ITSELF

Fran Tan

Where be sickness
If not here

How look naked
if not bare

When be time
if not now

Which be question
if not how

What keeps mind
if not free

Who breaks chains
if not me

Ten days back from Woodstock, so many roads, across, up and down America 'til a shot at college brought me back...I am walking up Eighteenth Avenue, just like I did when I was the kid on my way to the corner to meet the guys and see 'what's happening' – back when the street was our breath, we were its arms and I was always in some sort of shit.

I am as good as a stranger here now in this place I pushed away escaping – headed for a bus downtown to register for Fall Semester – 'Straight A's,' Editor of Literary Magazine, published Poet and candidate for a full scholarship at Harvard – Stoned on nothing but Peace, Love and Happiness – I will catch a train later for Belmar Beach – where my Flower Child Love, Candy and inner city Hippie Tribe are waiting in our Paradise by the Sea on that last long weekend of Summer 1969.

There...across the street, just up Melrose Avenue, Danny
Lavatola's father got his head blown off with a shotgun
pulling out of his garage before he could close the bullet-
proof window of his Continental...that big house on the
hill, fenced in like a fortress, still guarding his family. I
remember Danny's room and his clothes. Everything
was tailor made...in one closet, fifty shirts hanging, all
monogrammed silk...or fine cotton long-collar or high-
roll, the kind Sinatra wore. A wide closet full of suits,
sports jackets and pants in every shade of silk and silk
mohair stood across from another one, where cashmere
overcoats – black, blue and camel – silk mohair topcoats
in four colors, London Fog raincoats and lots of soft
leather jackets hung neatly...sets of well-shined Italian
loafers and wing-tipped flyweights sparkling from closet
floors and inside doors, beneath jammed tie and hat
racks next to a tall chest packed drawer after drawer
with perfectly folded Italian knit shirts, mohair sweaters
and alpaca sweaters. All socks are ribbed or sheer silk,
all underwear, silk boxers, monogrammed on the left leg
with the same initialing as shirts. On top, next to a large
bottle of Canoe, a jewelry box is filled with diamond
studded tie pins, gold and silver cufflinks, star sapphire
and diamond rings and a half dozen watches. Lying
like pick-up-sticks in another open box – a pile of
switchblade knives cover a 22, a Derringer and a
German Luger.
We were 14.
There was no outside world.

...across the street, on West End Avenue, was The Q-Stick
Lounge – now boarded up and empty – a pool room
on what was once our particular corner in Vailsburg –
an Italian-American ghetto full of such corners
in the West Ward of Newark:
a city full of gangs...

> *"What the fuck is he lookin' at!?" "Fuck is
> he lookin' at Goots!?" A very clean cut kid
> dressed collegiate style with a button-down
> plaid shirt, green khakis and penny loafers*

*just getting off the bus back from his first
day at Vailsburg High comes toward the
bench across from the Q-Stick where we are
hanging out. He doesn't look like us. He is
dirty blonde, wide blue-eyed and smiling
straight at me. Danny nudges me, scowling,
"Look at dis fuckin' geek!" Phillie Fantasia
bends into my ear, "What the
fuck is on his mind?" Carmine Peticchio
sitting at the end of the bench orders me,
"Hit him Goots...bang dis fuckin' jitterbug..."*

*I am looking into this kid's face. He is
getting ready to say "Hello." I am looking at
him, seeing someone from another planet – a
planet I would rather live on – where kids
don't get beat up for no reason. I want to
say hello. Danny is nudging me again.
Phillie is behind me whispering, "Bang dis
jitterbug Goots!" The kid passes in front of
me, carrying his books, smiling wider.
"What the fuck are you looking at!?" The
kid's face drops. I leap three quarters up
from my seat, kicking him in the chest,
scattering his books into the street, Danny
bangs him in the face, Frankie pounds him
in the stomach. The kid scrambles away,
crouched, holding his stomach, face
bleeding – Danny kicks his books down a
sewer, Carmine blurts, "Get the fuck out of
here you Fuckin' Jitterbug!" Phillie cracks
up.*

The kid would never be seen again.

...I pass the German Deli where Anthony
shot a uniformed cop right in front of the
place for not letting him cut ahead of him
at the Deli counter – then walked away
eating his sandwich, while me and Fran
Tan watched on from the corner...

Fran Tan lived on top of the Q-Stick. He disappeared a few years ago. I am thinking, maybe he is Groovin' somewhere out West. He would appear on that corner, as if a reminder that something *else* was going on – at the Q-Stick, or down South Orange Avenue, dressed to kill... just like everybody else, looking the part – just one of the guys...except he doesn't fight, doesn't hide and doesn't hustle. He is usually reading poetry aloud – mostly his own from a pad he always carries. He would ask what people *thought* about things – about...war, love, hate. No one knows what it's all about or why he is doing it, but he is always shown respect, like a priest or something...no one bothers him...he is too cool...*way* too cool.

Fran Tan is always the Messenger – the first Beatnik I know – gives me my first copy of 'The Prophet' – my first Phil Ochs album. He chants Peace and Love before the word Hippie is even around. He takes me to my first 'Be-In' and fills me in on what's happening on the West Coast.

... ...

Sat out on sidewalk of the Raydan Diner – front line lair of generations hostaged by birth to 'Family' rule – tied up tight with blood, starch and silk – one bare foot, thick skinned and dark with California Acid miles, is flat up, crossed lotus, as Uncle Allie – who last week advised my mother to kill me in my sleep – files by with the boys – slick and lawless – for their court of booths, bouffant broads, burgers and America. There is nowhere else to go, so I might as well be here – hair to my bare-chested beads – bellbottom – Indian vest – Just Being.

"What's on your mind?" Dennis, one of Uncle Allie's crew, threatens with the traditional signal I know because I was once one of them, could mean that I will be kicked bloody by the dozen legs of this mob creature passing around me. I flash up two fingers for peace – a sign to each of these prisoners of caprice I have known all my life and have known me, that I am free from their control. Artie, my age, stops the pack around me that is now tensed to go either way. In a second of hesitation loaded with the next decade, I notice his thumb hitched to a 'cowboy pocket' of his always tailor made silk mohair pants...and with an almost

groovy shaking of his smirked face – meant to display to The Boys that he is 'with it' – he utters the hippest thing he can come up with, "I'm not jumpin' into your bag" – directing the gang away from me and into the diner – intimating to me the true power of ideas, as he designates the caché of Cool more important than violence...and that **is** a brand new bag.

Frankie Fran Tan wheels slow in his Valiant, windows all open with four boss speakers and eight track tape blowing 'Fresh Cream' with 'suggested' highest volume, U-turn pulling up in front of the diner like a medicine wagon.

Fran Tan gives me his Look that means, "Dig this!" turning off the engine, leaving only **Cream:**

"Hey Hey heyeyheyYea! Hey hey hey heyey Yea," Jack Bruce megaphone mumbles 'rollin' tumblin'" speedball tongues working and wrecking Willie Dixon in rushes huckstering Blues verse incarnate at quick of electric raid Clapton solos noodle – winnowing rude and raw over Ginger Baker's shot siphoned thunder beating down – killing Chicago with wild child London invasion, declaring the latest Groove past the limit.

As tidal as San Francisco waved distortion – as siren as any hooked up mouth-harps blew in Windy City – from New York to London, to Liverpool, as ear bleeding loud as rhythm rockin' blues could get —— these guys were louder. Loud meant Sundance...loud meant 'move over rover' if you can't stand the Party...

"Bop Bah Bah Boo Bop Bah Bah Boo Bop Bah Bah Ba Boo Baaah... Who wants the-ah worry, the-ah hurr-ry of city life? Mah nee, nuthin' fah nee, we're wastin' the best of our life"

Fran Tan's Valiant is the only source for Sound impossible to get on hi-fi's built for Frankie Lane, standard equipped like refrigerators after ice boxes in every Italian American apartment on every Italian American block he cruises free delivering every summer night heavens exploding :

Sweet wine, hay making sunshine day breaking We can wait till tomorrow

Car speed, road calling, bird freed leaf falling
We can bide time
Bop Bah Bah Boo Bop Bah Bah Boo Bop Bah Bah Bah Boo Baaah

The car wiggles, stuffed with longhairs rolling stoned on
Clapton's massive moves, plucking the wind – slow hand riding it
over-amped and unimpeachable.

I am blessing Fran Tan for this spark and feel like splitting.
Maybe out to the coast again. Maybe New Mexico. Dennis eases
out from the diner and sticks his head into Fran Tan's front
passenger window with a sucker punch grin on.
"Hey-hey, Frankie Fran Tan! What's happening?"
Fran Tan gives him a nod, not disturbing his groove.
"Hey, Frankie...wanna turn the music down, Frankie boy?"
Fran Tan does not respond.
"Get this fuckin' shit out of here you fuckin' Hippie!"
Dennis lurches into the car window and rips the eight track tape
cartridge out, then throws it as high and far as he can across
South Orange Avenue. Fran Tan turns himself out of and around
the car straight into twice his size Dennis's face with a silent
stare that totally freaks Dennis out. He pushes Fran Tan up
against the car, wrestling him to the ground. In a moment, I am
between them. Without thinking, like reflex, I pop Dennis in the
face...and with that punch turn tables and pages in our lives.

In 14th Avenue Grammar School, I was tagged with a reputation
as a tough guy and had to act like one. I didn't know of anyone
who looked up to me...only Dennis. I knew and respected his
father. His father had been a boxer like mine. A quite man of
elegance, he always had a good word for me every time he
passed me on the street. A good word was a kind word. When
his son began to idolize me, I wanted to – put him on a different
path – get him away from the trouble – so every day, when he
tried to pal around with me, or run with my gang, I would pop
him in the face, he would cry and I'd tell him to GO HOME. My
psychology not having worked, he had grown up finding other
heroes not so reluctant in their roles and had gained a reputation
of his own – as an enforcer.

From the Raydan Diner, to the all the corners in quick distance, it
is announced that Dennis has called me out, challenging me to a

fight in the parking lot behind the Diner. I refuse and he yells from the parking lot "Punk!?" "Fuckin' Punk!" "Fuckin' Faggot!" into the night and enough to remind me who we both used to be. By the time I reach the parking lot, EVERYBODY, from Capo to Stooge is there, anticipating a fight that I realize, by their presence, has taken on a generational, cultural and political crucible that Dennis and I have been martyred to, not only by karma and chance, but by command. I stand there, chest to chest with the kid I punched around. He is bigger than me now and with such hatred in his face that I cry inside and see clearly by the crowd and his eagerness, that this is a big moment in his life and career. I can only match his emotion with silent memory of the faces he made chasing me, then crying in rejection.
"You know what I do to punks like you?!!"
"No I don't."
Bang! He wacks me in the cheek with all he has. The world is watching: the world that I left behind. A trial is on to attempt to discredit a Hippie Revolution – to save face for a bunch who have never recognized any force but their own... 'til now.
"You know what else I do to punks like you?"
"No."
He bloodies my lip with a left.
The crowd is moaning like an old cow.
"You know what else I do to punks like you?"
Encouraged and loose, he bangs me in the cheek with a hard right I flash the peace sign and leave the lot.
The next day it's all over the neighborhood that Dennis banged me and I punked out.

...and also that I didn't care.

And that was that.

... ...

Just as I reach the bus stop, a plain car screeches up onto the sidewalk catty-corner in front of me. Two men in plain clothes, one putting a 38 to my head, throw me up against a window, frisk me, handcuff me and push me into their car. They park back on the street while I.D.ing themselves as part of a new 'task force,' informing me that I am under arrest for possession of marijuana.

95

I don't have any Pot. When I protest, the blockhead driver waves two joints in front of me, "Then where did these come from, Pete?" I am surprised that he knows my name. I tell them that what they are doing is against the law. The driver turns a little closer and laughs in my face.

"You were busted two years ago in San Diego for possession. This is number two. You will do time." I feel the bottom drop out of any hope that they will cut me loose today. Everything I have done right has just been taken away by these two cowboy cops...WHY? When he sees that his threat has sunk in, the driver promises to "go easy on me," if I answer some questions – tell them what I know about a few people on their list. His overeager partner sitting shotgun, holds open a notepad and turns to me, eyes wet with anticipation and starts going down his list. I deny knowing each name.

Inside the terror of their trap, cursing Fate and nauseous with hatred for these pigs, I stare out the window
to a bench...
at a bus stop...
across from the boarded up
Q-Stick Lounge
...and I just about can see
Danny and Carmine and Phillie
just staring at me

... ...

It's a good vibe beautiful day on Belmar beach. Cathy is cutting my hair off in sections and handing each one over to Candy, who lays them in a basket – Tony Bono and his cousin Sarah are reading in turns from Lao Tzu – Bobby and Christine are strumming chords. The beach is full. No one notices our solemn ceremony, as I cut off my hair on advice from my Uncle Mike, who warns it is the only way I will stay out of jail.
and I am crying inside
for being halted in my glory
nabbed and branded
on that corner...
that corner
bloodied by a thousand crimes;

96

by a hundred lawless hoodlums
who no cops ever bothered —
what was my crime now?
...being a Hippie?

... ...

(Tomorrow, I will sit in a courtroom for hours – silk suit short hair
like its 1964 or something, trying to stay out of jail, as poor
blacks, some who were in my cell the week before and are still
there are sent back to those same cells, one after another, for
lack of bail
and I feel like standing up
and screaming about it
and letting them lock me up again too
because it is so wrong
and because it is so unfair
and because the whole time
Uncle Mike rushes
from judge to lawyer to detective
still lobbying and arranging my sentence,
these poor blacks
are being confined
without being convicted
or even charged...
and by the time I step up before the judge,
everyone is looking at each other signifying —
the prosecutor — the judge — my uncle —
and it is all prearranged
and nothing to do with justice –
just like my arrest had nothing to do with law –
as I stand there ready to erupt and blow it all
and they are all still signifying and wondering
what I am going to do
and it's all set...
all I have to do is plead Guilty
and the judge looks me dead in the eye
and I do...
and they cut me loose.)

... ...

Candy picks my hair from the basket, tossing one bunch at a time into the ocean. We stand knee deep in the water. As the waves crash in and the tide rolls out to other lands, I see the storm Nixon and his vengeful, jealous henchmen will put on all of us and on the Hippie Movement – proved in the stirring memory of a friend – in his knowing poems when nobody knew – and in the bleak irony of the first name on the Pig's list:

Franco Frantantoni...

Frankie Fran tan...

Fran tan.

Fillmore

burnt out day off
bar-tending
Uptown crippled of Chic –
rashed of banality –
overexposed of Powder
postpartum-mortem
Studio 54 Eurotrash crowds
clamoring,

I walk deliberate slow
in gray-black isolation suit
expecting no hint of Muse long estranged
one block worn as next –
trying to find My Country
down 2nd Avenue
to East 6th Street,
no expectations –
empty as the
boarded-up tight
building I straddle –
sped by the bubbled poster layer/
graffiti'd/black-white
slop-stacked palate
of pre-gentrified East Village,
1979.

East 6th & 2nd –
just another trash corner
to just pass like any other,
spying dirty men
drunks pissing
junkies copping
junkies hanging
and the occasional police chase

East 6th & 2nd
vacancy shrouded –

just another corner to pass...
no hint, sense or ghost
of a past...nor the
Crossroads Palace
it once famously showcased:
The Fillmore East...

marquee gone
lobby walled-in,
silent as forgotten...

'til chain clank
stops me in my tracks
turning onto East 6th
and I step inside
The Great Hall
for the first time in ten years,
climbing through the side doors
wide open...

the side doors we used to line Lucky...
the side doors – special times cracked
enough to peek over-amped yardbird
quicksilver majestic beginning,
before The Entire Globe tuned in –

the side doors – wide open this time –
hanger gates to motor shovel destruction
readying first big money Gay Disco 'The Saint'...

one bulldozer squeals like twisting steel left,
the other grinds smoking right,
passing each other distributing mounds of earth –
brash churning plunking abandon swash
of construction-site Destiny rattle,
leveling with haste
ground consecrated in Groove –
digging over under sideways down
waving dunes of Rushes Flashing me Back
from row 60 to front –
Hey Day hugging this emptiness audience
arranged me:

Buddy Guy standing right next to me
blowing Real electric blues for 15 minutes,
Wicked Picket Grin – before
Traffic's first...never much further away,
Albert or B.B. before Hendrix or Cream
Or Who...later Beck Mayall Ten Years After
Tull...Sonny Brownie Staples
Before Band Miles or Joni before Buckley
...Hammond to Cocker to Santana –
Canned Heat Moby Grape with Byrds
or Janis...Havens come Steppenwolf
come Butterfield...Creedence come
Winter come Zeppelin – always 3 on a bill –
$3, $4 or $5, 'til 3, 4 or 5a.m....
when The Airplane leaves the stage Triumph! –
Maria Callas piped in tremolo ogle
'no more encores' signal –
All lights turned-up full
tilting room smoky golden –

Night Over

...the balcony is gone –
all that remains are
the white marble balustrade
sturdy in place
demanding the vision
of the heaven's gate foyer and
swooned orchestra it once separated...

and the mammoth, 12 foot high stage opposite
now aching pitch black
– nude of Light Show and curtain –
a stark, sharp monolith of raw potency
cantilevered above the dirt piles
the dozers heap, then push even –
under the mother orb opera house chandelier
still imposed overhead – a rubbed lightning archive
of Rock & Roll Glory,
now crusted opaque in demolition dust.

... ...

the façade burnt down
during a Who concert

Bill Graham threw
a big goodbye concert –
West Coast/East Coast bands...
and The Allman Brothers...

and that was that

done

finished.

...too much going on
to Celebrate...
too much too bad too fast
too Trouble too Nixon.

The Bold Heart
of Peace & Love
ripped out at Kent State –
Hippies licking wounds
in exile –
Music, no longer brave
enough to Feed
nor Protect.

so, The Fillmore goes out –
like a bakery
or a men's shop
or a 5&10 –

only quicker –

like a secret
or a pipedream
or a myth...

yet, out those side doors,
jumping back onto E. 6th –
I recall with singular Joy,
how hip-happy-sad
I was, right there,
when the world
was on my shoulders –
Blasting!

Bag

the chair
has an open bag on it
from Woodstock grocery

the bag blocks
part of a Matisse print
that formerly hung over
a television in Gramercy Park
for 25 years
on a lacquered brick wall
in the living room
of a rent controlled
big one bedroom
ground floor apartment
with a garaged townhouse
next door
and a cheese shop
across the street
in a quiet section
without a nightclub
or a hot restaurant –
inoculated from bustle
by every single need
in walking distance –
Tall with Survival
ready to turn '70s to '80s
Downtown in a Hungry City
Desperate to Spend
on sleepy places lulled deaf
to errant gentry whistles
on the steps of their
neighborhood funeral

JFK & Me

Kal Katz entered
the men's room
at lunchtime
while I was in
the stall successfully
getting myself back
into my high-wasted suit pants
after peeing...
He said to an acquaintance
who was drying his hands,
"Strong, no?" I guessed
referring to the smell of
my urine after a long night
closing...maybe they were
talking about something else –
either way – I was hoping that
they did not recognize my shoes.
Kal was always jovial and most
days in his midget baseball cap –
the kind very rich people wear
sailing.
I always looked at him as old
because he was gray and exuded
Erudite and ease with authority – but
he wasn't much older than me –
just in a completely different set –
he lunched
with Jackie Kennedy
from time to time.
I gave them Table 43,
from where they could see
and not be seen...
looking back, I think
they were an item

Jackie Kennedy
once speeded her
step across the parking lot
at Martha's Vineyard Airport
until she was right in my face
all lit up
at just the moment
I had to turn away to get back
in my car.

My floor manager
told me that she saw
Jackie Kennedy
project a foot long stream
of clear snot from her nose,
then snort it right back up
without batting an eyelash,
before anyone else could
notice, on her way out
of a Garden Room
publishing luncheon.

I once served John Jr.
a Ginger Ale at Caroline's
30th Birthday Party...
he looked at me from
across the bar
packed with all the loneliness
I could imagine – alive with the tragedy
I hoped I was happy
to see him enough not to hint at,
as he turned, adoring his sister –
all dressed-up and dancing with
her friends.

I walked out
on bail from
a Federal Courtroom
in Manhattan
with my bloody overcoat
over a hospital gown – head
bandaged and limping –

looked up and the first
thing I saw was John Jr.'s
eyes gazing at me – him dapper
heading into the commissary.
He recognized me.

I saw my Sicilian born and raised
father, for the first and only time,
up late at night listening to
a bedside radio. He stayed up
until he heard the 1960
Democratic National Convention
nominate JFK.

I got a penny in my change
with JFK's profile pressed
into it between Abraham Lincoln's
neck and the mint date. I saved it
until it was somehow lost in
a renovation 40 years later. I found
out recently, calling an NPR coin
expert that they were common
and maybe worth $2.

My first essay was "John F. Kennedy –
Humanitarian or Politician?" in which
I documented him swerving his car
dangerously to avoid hitting a squirrel
on Nantucket.

Alan Young, glassy eyed jumping,
came bounding down the steps
into sophomore High School cafeteria,
spitting on my sleeve as his head
whipped my way with a smile-wide
nervous giggle, yelping:
"Kennedy Got Killed!!!
Kennedy Got Shot!!!
They Shot Him In Texas
With Machine Guns!!!
Johnson Is Dead Too!!!"

Thus, the first iteration
of America's broken heart
pavane – still somber.

Shizuko Yamamoto used
JFK's picture as an example
of Sanpaku Eyes at
the first East-West Center
we built near Time Square.

The last time I saw John Jr.
was just before lunch time.
He was walking fast down
W. 55th Street...I guessed on his way
to 'La Côte Basque.' I stepped
out to the sidewalk from my
Maître'd podium and said,
"Come Back."
He turned, recognizing me again
and said, "I will, I will."

I Miss You Like A Bone
(to Pete)

When I Walk
I Drop My Left Foot Sometimes
Tripping Into Your Laughter...

I Even Hurt Myself
A Few Times

No One
Knew Us

Only Us

Now Only Me

I Wipe Every Day Clean
Like We Were –

– Quick Like We Were –

– Young Like We Were –

Each
Breaking Beloved

Papa Pasta Fazool

"jab jab jab
Left, right LEFT!
jab jab jab
right
left
Right!
use your knees...
Hook!
cover your face...
jab jab jab!
right jab jab jab...
Keep Your Jab Up Peter!..."

His gentle laugh at my awkward
attempts keeps me trying...

'Kid Galahad'
Breadwinner
first son
with 7 sailed from Sicily
no way back
back when

8 rounds 50 times,
3 rounds 200 times,
if he won
he got a gold watch
he pawned...
if he lost
he got nothing...
his only luck,
his Southpaw...
guess that is what
'Hall of Fame'
is all about

Keep Moving!
...Right Left Right

Uppercut! Relax...
My Birthday 7
got real trunks
Guinea-T to match
1st sneaks

he sits on stool
facing me
mitt on each hand
fielding each punch he calls for

Kind Quiet Boxer
hashing out the Rules of
the Game, step by punch
under the stairwell of
common hallway...step by punch...
the only thing he knew –
never anything else to
show me or say
years turn decades turn long lives
gloves off
strangers.

Now, as I see him in last room
to witness his last event
featured for no crowd
in last hospital bed –
mismatched, battling way up weight
contender Pugilistic Dementia

– jaw open/close cranking
dry tongue gibbered mumble/stutter
non-stop neck-swivel head roll
light eye pallor
contort jump up
jammed back
strapped-down
sequence-same –
over and over and over
ruthless hour to hour...

12th Round coming to an end...

no one except me would have remembered
his short, sly laugh when I snapped a jab
or cracked a right...
now, at my final face look
at his incomprehensible
incomprehensibly
pummeled existence,
I say what I know:
"Keep Your Jab Up Dad!"...
and for the very splitest of seconds
clear as a bell
I hear from deeper than the
strung-out babble of dying,
that same gentle/sly laugh –
the one
I now inherit and revel –
closet full of Birthday Trunks
lined up.

... ...

Ingredients:

1 14 oz. can Cannellini Beans
1½ cups Ditalini pasta
12 canned plum tomatoes
(water drained/tops removed)
1 rib of celery chopped fine
1 small carrot chopped fine
1 small yellow onion chopped fine
4 cloves of garlic minced
¾ cup chopped fresh Italian parsley
1 quart of chicken stock
2 cups of water
1 dry bay leaf
Kosher salt
fresh ground black pepper
hot pepper seeds
grated Parmigiano

······ ······ ······

add olive oil to heated pot
add vegetables, garlic and bay leaf,
sauté, turning over medium heat
for 4 or 5 minutes as you sprinkle
¼ tsp. Kosher salt and ¼ teaspoon
fresh ground pepper into the pot,
adjusting heat so that nothing burns.

add beans with their liquid and chicken
stock to pot, turning heat up to high,
as you stir bring soup up to rapid boil.

add Ditalini and cook at steady medium
boil until pasta is cooked 'al dente'
(about 8 minutes)

remove from heat and let set.

sprinkle ½ teaspoon red pepper seeds
into a soup bowl
ladle in Pasta Fazool
top with 2 tablespoons
of grated Parmigiano
finish with the rest of
chopped parsley

······ ······ ······

My father never cooked this meal.

He did learn to make a good fried egg
Guam, Okinawa, China Marine.

I Stand In Hidden Light.

Anguish Escarole

Ingredients:

1 medium head of escarole
½ pint cherry tomatoes
10 pitted, ripe black olives
7 garlic cloves
olive oil
½ teaspoon red pepper seeds
salt

----

cut off one inch from the bottom
of escarole head
pull each escarole leaf off
and rinse under cold water
until clean of sand and dirt,
place cleaned leaves in a
large colander to drain

(recalling ingénue-soon star
doing same once upon a time,
belting hilarity
between belted show tunes
[almost] cleaning
the pirouette plucked leaves in
slow low water pressure
West Village tenement)

turn colander until water
is mostly drained.
slice each leaf lengthwise, straight down
the center of its stalk – then slice those
pieces in half lengthwise again,

(like Gaetano's blind wife did
on Sullivan Street
on that Perfect Summer Night

when we were in love
and the old soldier
you tended bar to
at Milady's
invited us home to dinner)

place leafs
back in colander

smash garlic cloves
with the flat side of a knife,
discard skins and cut off the gray ends
then press with knife into chunky paste

slice cherry tomatoes in half

pour 3 tbsp. olive oil into heated pan,

(expectant, like we were on Martha's Vineyard,
'house party' cooking
for designer Andre' and friends)

add garlic and pepper seeds
turn for 2 minutes.

add cherry tomatoes and ¼ tsp. salt

(and yes, smell Naples! – ride high to
Firenze, then Groove Cinque Terre to Aix
...your laughter crackling convertible Whoosh!)

cover and lower heat.
cook for 7 minutes

(memory numbed
from the pain
of your betrayal)

uncover and turn up heat.
add escarole and olives
sprinkle with ¼ tsp. salt,
turning constantly for
5 minutes as

escarole sizzles

(all the while singing
"Sweet Becky Walker"
at the top of lungs)

cover and lower heat
to percolating boil

cook for 5 minutes sanguine.

turn off heat
set aside half-covered for 2 minutes.

serve in a large soup bowl
to yourself
– Alone –

(Feel It...like that day
in Union Square Station)

on the way back from Timbuktu
----
on the way back from Timbuktu
I saw you
passing the other way
on a platform
across two tracks
on a different line
you looked mean
and desperate

we locked eyes
just as your train
pulled in
then out

as if we weren't
man and wife

The Cat

"Wrhuhuhereheah!" A paw whacks hard, flat and deliberate against my cheek. I turn sides and bunch myself up. "Wrherhrahukereah!" Again, a cold smack from the paw. Philippe has never spoken to me this way before, nor has he ever been so calculated with his paws. He is trying to talk to me! If he can't accomplish that, he will certainly wake me up with that jabbing paw; "Wrherhrahukereah!" Whack!

It's early. I got home late last night from a Halloween party at a National Lampoon cartoonist's loft where he chided me for possessing the "useless condition" of Humility. After that I sat under a fifteen foot high painting of his for three hours, talking with Timmy, my estranged wife's best friend. The painting depicted a mythical helmeted conqueror with his spear through a huge cobra – a castle in the background – he had saved the day. All night I've been dreaming of snakes. Blap! "Awaaahwrrr!" "Let me sleep!"

... ...

It's mid-seventies West Village. I'm living in Miles Davis' old half-sunken studio in the landmark 'Twin Towers' apartment building on Bedford Street. Built in the '30s by a Dutch architect as a residence for artists, it still houses a card deck full of painters, writers, dancers and actors. Each apartment in The Towers is of a completely different hand-hewed design, a gesture celebrating individuality. My apartment's particular eccentricity is a wall of showcase windows half submerged beneath street level. This gives me a grand view of unsuspecting automobile passengers, hubcaps, dogs, cats and small children lining up for school directly across the street, where the inscription engraved above the school playground reads – "CHILDHOOD SHOWS THE MAN."

My first week there, in bed with the young actress who will soon become my wife...it must be 4 a.m. ...I'm awakened by chains clanking and metal clicking in the alleyway above – just outside our door. As the door begins to thump, I get real nervous and go for my knife from Nazareth on a shelf behind the bed. I nudge Elise awake, alerting her to the situation. She lifts her head, listening for 5 seconds, then tells me to go back to sleep. How can she be so blasé? There are two men with weapons prying at our door! For the next half hour I lie on guard, alone with the problem...with a sleeping beauty to protect. I listen to the chiming of metal against chain. The door pushes against the lock with an eerie rhythm as the men whisper outside. Then, suddenly, the marching sounds of heavy boots back out the alleyway. I hear a man's voice clearly, "That was lovely." The boots return to the street and go separate ways – one pair toward Grove Street and one pair toward Christopher Street. A few hours later, daylight breaks and I have been up in a staring stupor for hours and finally figure out what had happened out there, I eagerly lay my theory out to a waking Elise. She laughs in my face. MY, I have been away for a while.

The West Village then is basically still a neighborhood of small shops and old-timers. The gays have Christopher Street while the second wave yuppies invade Grove Street and landlords try everything short of murder to uproot rent control tenants and long-time merchants, to clear room for the high first rents and trendy restaurants to feed the invading suburban kids. On Carmine Street the Italian street gangs rule, Andy Warhol can still be seen being helped across Barrow Street or in Sheridan Square, moving slowly, in a long recovery from Valerie Solanas' bullet. The old 'Speak,' Chumley's is a local hangout; at The Duplex and Marie's Crisis Cafe, cabaret is free every night. Sweet Basil has just opened, Ron Carter, Kenny Burrell and the Brecker Brothers jam there three nights a week to half-filled houses. Down at Arthur's Tavern, Mabel sings Dinah Washington and raps out Art Tatum on her piano, then jazzmen from all over town gather after their gigs for after hour, closed door, very hot jams. Jessica Lange is the toughest waitress at the Lion's Head and Philippe Petit performs his ferocious one-man circus from a chalk circle he draws on the sidewalk, stringing his tightrope taut across it from the steel posts of parking signs. Distant bongos still cut the night, as gentrification is about to roll over this part of town like a Sherman tank.

But what can I say about what's going on in America now anyway? What do I remember of it except what I **want** to remember of it – its young majesty and bold beauty from coast to coast a dozen times on so many roads, hitching or driving an old Ford or Dodge into the ground on the way to L.A. or Frisco. That's about it. Now, after returning from years and thirty countries, to me, America seems uniquely inhospitable to its own citizens – cruel to its young and cruel to its old, while, uncannily, the world looks on with envy. What do I know about New York City – me an expatriate exiled back to his own yard? All I know about this corner of the United States is that the air is poison and the people unnecessarily tough – obsessed with self-defense and trained like dogs to shut themselves down at the hint of inspiration or compassion...but here in the Village, I feel safe and as restless as I get, I thrive on this happy/sad parade from the Hudson River to Washington Square.

I walk my cat on a leash through the neighborhood. He is famous. Everyone calls him by his name: Philippe. I named him after my friend, Philippe Petit, because the cat could balance himself while running on all fours across skinny exposed pipes in the apartment and also for his absolute bravery in facing down and bagging troupes of water bugs the size of mice. He is a funny looking thing, Philippe is... beautiful...a handsome devil...but ODD...eight inch whiskers sticking out and flying up, as if individually waxed, from a button nose and the most curious, paranoid black eyes...a streak of pure white curls up one side of his upper lip, down his whole chin, then gushes to the bottom of his chest in a perfect "V," looking like a white beard against the long, black hair that drapes the rest of his body like a dust mop right to the ground, hiding his legs. His huge hairy tail stands straight up like a pole, a foot and a half high by four inches wide, each hair stiff horizontal as if electrified. No one knows what he is – a skunk? a lynx? a new type of Chinese dog?

The secret to his flubadub pedigree lay hidden in a shed near a frozen pond on a farm in a lonely rural corner of Northeast Connecticut, where Elise and I had gone to visit an old friend of mine, Tina, her new husband, and their daughter. It was there that I found Philippe one sunny winter's day – abandoned, the size of a hardball, hair frizzed straight out like a pom-pom, screaming as loud as he could peep. How he got there, I don't know... how I got there is another story. When I received the invitation to visit that farm I hesitated, but it would at least get us out of the city for a few days. We should have nothing to fear. Elise and I were quite in love and immune to any bullshit...even if it was Tina.

... ...

Sitting in the late night kitchen of this woman, somewhere in Connecticut. Tina has put her husband and daughter to bed, worn Elise out with conversation obsessive and now has me to herself as she hovers across the table, spinning our far from happy relationship years earlier in Europe into some sort of "good old days" fable, while professing her continuing love for me. I try to be polite. She sees through it and is not pleased. I begin to be bombarded by sharp electric jolts to my heart. I have felt this before in the presence of certain people. I used to feel it from Tina from time to time. At first, I thought of it as some kind of psychological disorder which crippled me and prevented me from carrying on a decent conversation. Over the years, I came to understand the force as emanating from outside of me – a kind of lightning I was being hit with that I had no defense against: Shaktipat – electro-magnetic force – exploding at my heart, jolting me like shock treatment. For what purpose? Perhaps to open up my heart chakra, blasting through the thick shell of protection I had built around it surviving, to free its energy to flow in me and through me. But this was something extreme. Shock after shock hits me with every breath Tina takes, till I am bent over, forehead on the table, holding my heart, wondering if I will make it. I look up at Tina and ask her, "Are you trying to kill me?" She looks placidly down to me and says "I don't know what it is – I just feel it coming through me..." I don't trust her. I know that she is letting it through. It doesn't matter where it comes from, anyway...only that it stops – that my heart chakra is blown open – and that I have never felt it attacked since.

Tina ends the night restless and informs me that she is tired of messing around – she intends to study the Black Arts. I guess I am supposed to be scared or concerned. I only feel pity for her once again – as she abuses her sensibilities – pretty dolls she rips the heads off of and tosses across her mirror padded cell. Tina's psychic gluttony reminds me why I abhor her. Her total neglect of Elise and the way she second-rates her husband and child is sickening. The next day, we end the weekend walking out into the sunny frozen woods behind their farm. They swear, "It's on a ley line." Elise and I are plenty ready to head back to the City. We will probably never see these people again. We hear some strange squealing coming from an outhouse near a frozen pond. Elise and Tina go over and find two tiny baby kittens abandoned and freezing. One is a tabby and one is this odd-looking creature with an almost human, white-bearded face and huge whiskers sunken in a round puff of frizzed hair – Philippe. He rides back to New York City on my shoulder, Elise and I singing "Sweet Becky Walker," in perfect harmony all the way down to Sheridan Square.

... ...

Elise runs from theater company to theater company somewhere in the middle of it we get married, go to Europe on a long honeymoon, where she decides that she is sick of the acting and we decide that when we return, I will go for a career in the Healing Arts – we will leave New York City and start a new life. But the minute we get back, Elise maniacally dives into Variety Backstage street pound pounding like we had never met or talked about anything else and I see her where she needs to be and we stay put...

I go from 'mature' busboy to manager at Mr. William Shakespeare's Pub, where it seems to me and everyone else I know that we are the 'perfect couple' as she screws every lead actor and every director of every company and has always done that and I never know it till she really starts to feel different inside and gets herpes in weird places and then starts ordering #16 – General Tang's Chicken with cashews from take out – ...#16? then there's a 10% doubt in my mind... then 50, as I'm watching her...

then 75 when she comes to work at Shakespeare's at the door strutting her stuff and I don't know her and finally, when it's 95, but I still can't believe it I ask her and she cries hysteric with guilt and conflict.

my world –
the world I tried to create
for myself in this new/old world
I am orphaned to –
falls apart,
exposed in the wake of a howling Devil, as it splits my
tenement – leaving the winter freeze for warmth
and I kick Elise out when she can't stop
and leave her shit on the street
when she won't pick it up
and am thrown
into a tumble of despair
that can easily kill me
with guys coming out of the woodwork
signifying there are more
who have fucked her
... perhaps to defuse the anger
I think of killing her lover with.

       I've got a choice:
       get depressed
       or party into this strung out City

       I know depression doesn't work
       or else it would have worked,
       so I try the other
          and waggle
          in the hungry wind,
          with enough cocaine and
          gratification to keep me occupied
          through the storm
          and still frozen

can't meditate any more or tell anyone in my family
because my mother has become sick and they say
this time she will die and I don't want to bother anyone with my
troubles but finally call my brother, who leaves a message
too late, that mother is calling for me...

       as I lose my wife, my mother and nearly
       myself that cold, cold winter, alone

122

"Urghaghgh!" "Uraleheh!" Blap! "Urgglleerah!" Blap! Blap! What is it with this cat today? Has he gone crazy? Do cats get rabid? Maybe he misses Elise. After all, this was our cat – a cat who used to sit on my shoulder and cuddle up in Elise's face back when he was tiny and Elise and I still had a marriage going. A cat who I will later give Elise custody of when she moves to Hollywood with her comedian lover. A cat who they will use for talk show chit-chat joke material as I am forced by media every time I turn on the set to connect with their fame circuit and affair. {He marries her, then dumps her two years later.}

"Baryahah!" "Uryllkh!" Blap! Smack! I'm waking up now. I've been dreaming of snakes all night. I say to myself, "There's a snake under the bed." Blap! "Urghgh!" I jump out of bed cursing Philippe banging at the trash can as if it is his enemy. I move the trash can and an 8-foot boa constrictor curls its head straight up and at me!!! Holy shit! This is not supposed to happen here! This is not the jungle! This is the Village! I take the bar from my police lock and prod the snake up and out into the alleyway. I'm standing there in my drawers – the snake hissing like a radiator – as I keep it at bay with the police bar. People are coming down into the alley on their way to work. They seem mystified by the scene. They continue on their way without a blink. Finally, my next door neighbor, a piss queen and disc jockey at The Mineshaft, sticks his yellow head out his door informing me that Berta the ballet dancer in 3A had a pet snake once. He goes up and fetches Berta, a Goldie Hawn lookalike. She runs overjoyed down to the alley, lifts the snake around her shoulders, cuddling its hoary head to her lips, squealing, "Harold! I love you, Harold! I missed you so much, Harold!"

Yes, this IS the Village. Harold had escaped from his tank in Berta's bedroom a few months earlier and slithered through the guts of the Twin Towers before resurfacing under my bed on that particular morning. Philippe, my beautiful mutt had saved my life and returned the long-vanished Vengeful Serpent to its pit.

Profiterole Sauvage

Ingredients: there ain't no more

Albert's Elbow

I've got to go up to Polo on 72ⁿᵈ St. to pick out uniforms. Sixty dollar shirts, thirty dollar ties for the waiters, hundred-ten dollar pants, three hundred-fifty dollar jackets for floor managers. It's a nice, early Spring day. At 57ᵗʰ St., I head North on Madison – neighborhood of the free, home of the brave and the very not so inclined – prime time preserved here in twenty square block storm-eye secure free delivery stacked Pentagon of movers and shakers. I plan to walk straight up past Le Relais and take a fast look. It's been tough years recovering from that place. I can still hear Albert yelling in my ear something I can't really understand but must heed immediately. I can still feel the Rush of rushes twisting in and around the hook of the tiny bar. I remember the Quiet – sitting at a stripped metal table left out at the corner of the sidewalk terrace for us after closing on the rare Sunday night we weren't swept up all over town partying hard – Albert sitting there at his table, puffing away, goofing on 'The World' – 'The Whole Chic World' who showed up regularly and ready for anything at <u>his</u> *bistro – squeezing his cigarette flat puffing away between long belly laughs – a man at the top of his Game – living the untouchable life he aimed for – allowing no compromise.*

I remember the waiters, Gerard, Frank, Jan, Jimmy, Christian, John, Luc, Dorian, Gabriel, Richard – half of them very French and able to edict their snobbery in that very French enclave – the other half, American studs cashing in, each of whom, rumor had it, Albert had slept with – all, fabulous prototypes for a coming generation of 'She-She' hangouts. On the floor, black vested formal, they pace the imperceptible hustle characteristic of every classic: the warming hum of success. In five years of loaded cues slipped between clips of the crowd banging for attention, each one of them taught me something different about 'the business,' high signed through a shutter snapped text of camaraderie and jerking joie de vivre, too fleeting to record – too instant to predict – too busy to stop mining for more than a second the cash mother lode we had cracked.

Dressed up like waiters with doll heads, the Chinese busboys,
quick, quiet and invisible as breeze, clearing and setting each
table like a stage – half a dozen times a day – kung-fu exact – as
they mass their 20% fortunes sent over long seas to their
homeland, where Relais has made them barons. The fiefdom of
the kitchen – the chef – the sous – the garde manger – THE
SYSTEM – the franchise Française, rolling out the standard:
Gigot, Roquefort Endive, Ronons Sauté, Blanquette de Veau,
Steak au Poivre, Mousse Pâté, Coq au Vin, Cold Poached Salmon
Hollandaise, Monkfish to Saucisson, Pot au Feu to Paillard,
Raspberries and Crème Anglaise, Tarte Tatin, Profiterole to
Napoleon – flying out tout de suite and veet to famished
customers gobbling Paris as fast as we can plate, serve and pour.

I remember going home with three thousand dollars in hundred
dollar bills I forgot I had rolled up in my socks because there was
no more room in the cash drawer and no time to run upstairs and
stash it in the office. Two days later – my next shift – when I
returned the money, I found that no one knew it had gone
missing. There was so much cash being collected, no one could
keep track of it...so much coke, none could finish it.

... ...

Albert is up on top of the best table in the house, smack in the
middle of the rectangle, his legs compassed, improbably
balancing him over the petite flower arrangement, as he spins
and dives – an action painter at his canvas – into the poor
freaks stuck like pins on the plush maroon velvet cushions
beneath him. Clamping it on either side with clenched, sweaty
fists, he stretches and shoves his little bistro menu, wrapped in
clear plastic jacket, close into each of their faces, spitting and
groaning his comically bad English, as he attacks them, nostrils
flaring, with a 'translation' of the French they cannot read.

"Tis isz bick *cowwnt* you can leeek for appeatizzair, heh, heh
heh." Then around to one of the girls, between harrowing
taunts, "Tis isz nize caak you can try for your assz." On, on and
around, spitting and rasping. "Tis isz bick dildo waiter can
faaack you wheat, no? Heh, heh, heh heeeeeeh."

Barbara Walters and her producer are dining two feet to Albert's left. Across the room behind Albert, the first President of Namibia and his diamond smuggling agent are under huge, heavy gilded mirrors. Down the wall is Peter O' Toole and guests, then Raquel Welch, daughter and husband, next to Henry and Mrs. Kissinger, next to Jackie O, next to Michael Bennett, next to Halston. Ivan Lendl is there...Jerry Hall, her sisters and friends, dress that corner against the frosted glass paned splash dividing the bar from the restaurant, while Esme and four other top models huddle at the opposite wall, next to that side's line up – Jacqueline Bisset, Stockard Channing, Donald Sutherland, Mariel Hemmingway, Liza Minelli, Charles Aznavour – all plugged in under identical oversized mirrors – almost rubbing shoulder to shoulder – glance to glance – horseshoeing back to Barbara Walters and Albert's exhibition on the main table that 'L's' out into to the center of the room, separating 'the front' from 'the back', where ducking ambassadors, ministers and congressmen, cigar chewing raiders, gallery owners, fifth generation upper East Side affluent, every French restaurateur eating crow, big shot nobodies and fawning curious are seated, peeking the ultimate 'people watch' from 'Siberia,' provided as well as concealed in glimpses the tall mirrors angled out from the walls spray in opposition to every sharp angle, as a spattering of Kennedy's, Mellons, Astors and Paces rub with Grimaldis, Rothschilds and a dozen fixtured barons, princes, princesses and exiles, fueling a hurrying parade of food, smashing glasses and expensive smoke, in this frontier colonial clutter of clashing liaisons.

At the bar, pressed gossip scavengers try to contain themselves, the young and beautiful line up to be explored and examined, oil caliphs and magnates from Gulf, to equator, raging garmentos out of their element, head-fat brokers, renegade bankers, Sardinians, movie stars, everyone Hollywood hot for the moment, socialites and rock idols schmoozing – wiseguys and con men on their best behavior – all – tossing new money and cocaine, while *every* leftover from the just smacked down slammed shut Studio 54, drinks all day and all night, half of them on Albert. Local and international tricks of every persuasion sparkle or snarl, looking on from their webs at one or another of the little cafe tables set across from the bar, while, *tout le jour*, the doors frame the exhibition, folded boldly open onto Madison Avenue, where the limos jockey for space, prized tables are set on an 'anything goes' sidewalk...and New York learns a new way to party.

"Maybe you like *meee* for deeezsairt! Heh heh heh heh heeeeeeh," he switches abruptly – starting on the long-haired blonde guy – with completely demonic, commanding deep throat guffaw draining into phlegmy cough before he starts again, "Maybe you like nyesze banannn?!" pointing between his legs with the menu, addressing the room with fierce Harpo clown eyes he unleashes, brushing back, with his nearly burned down cigarette hand, the brunette sheep dog Dennis the Menace bang covering his eyes. He is up on that table roaring before the chic world, where no one can deny Albert his pillage, nor his crown of outrageousness.

I knew something was going to happen when, in the middle of it all – a screaming Saturday night at Relais – these four, rich by whatever, faux Hippie types from Atlanta had walked in, New Mexico silver and turquoise strapped, buckles hanging, perfect clean jeans, two thousand dollar suede fringe jackets, one of a kind cowboy boots, long hair coiffed sloppy – they come from a place where they must be *it* – to Relais – *without a reservation* – directly in to the swept smooth pit of Albert's coliseum.

Albert takes one look at them, hears their serious, near cracker drawl and pounces on them, escorting them immediately in – *slowly* – making sure everyone notices his catch. When he sits them at Madam La Grange's banquet, (where she can be found every Sunday, low, low cut buxom, one foot long cleavage tits, displaying at least two million dollars in alternately all ruby and diamond or all emerald and diamond ostentatious masterpieces on that chest, on her fingers and on her wrists, flanked stiffly by Arab body guards beneath her divan sized breasts and high, bright red, Marie Antoinette hairdo) – *the main banquette* – the middle of the room showcase facing out toward the bar and the street...when he pushes that table back locking them in, I know it can't be long before the fireworks start.

Dorian the Perfect, Gay courtesan from L.A., who has not aged in a dozen years thanks to sponsors and surgeons, one of the five non-French waiters here allowed the privilege, arrives at the table. I can read the trepidacious complicity in his stance. He knows he is going to have to deal with Albert soon and is getting ready to duck. He hands out the menus with his typical Lori Anderson big smile, fluttering when the two Southern couples can't read it in the French it is written in and ask him to translate.

From the banquette behind them, facing the rear of the restaurant, where he has sat disguising himself as occupied, garrulously entertaining a thrilled group of East-Siders, treating them merely to ensure his proximity, lurking to pounce – where I have been watching his smoke swirl and eyes dart in survey – laying for the opportunity he has now found – Albert twists up from his aisle seat, tie skewing, Valentino shirt collar popping its tips straight out from his Valentino couture lapels struggling to maintain their form, as he whorls a hairpin curve around to stage center, ripping a menu from Dorian's now trembling hand and presents himself before the poor customers, growling and spitting at the two couples like an angry beast until their hair stands up, visible from a distance.

"You wunt trunszzlayshown???! I givf you trunszzlayshown!" In one motion, without breaking his knees, flying like a devil, Albert flings his small to medium self onto their table, landing – plop! – directly in the center and balanced...without a glass breaking, a plate flipping and barely a jingle of silver...as if he does it every day. Then the bludgeoning starts, met with the slightest turn of every head in the restaurant, no one showing concern or amusement lest the show be abbreviated – no one prepared to ever leave – Barbara Walters close enough to get wet...and I figure, publicity-wise, we have had it.

"Maybe you like one plate of *camm* to begin! – No! – heh heh heh heh heh...or maybe *you* like to try one banannn?!" to one of the girls. It goes on for four or five minutes, until Albert drops down from the table with the sweaty, jackal's smirk that I have become unintentionally used to; like he has just ripped flesh and is looking for a cigarette. The crackers get up and leave, boot heels clomping and the almost silence the spectacle has attenuated slips immediately back to the normal – 'Ooowh' – 'Aaahh' – 'Oh!' – 'Voila!' – 'Aha!' – coo crescendo clatter of rich and famous.

Albert turns to the bar, face on and off revealed in Cubist 'Noir' portion formed amidst billows of sharp smelling smoke he exhales. One shirttail nearly out, tie swinging like a pendulum, open jacket flapping obnoxious as his strut, his low snicker almost drooling with guttural satisfaction, "Heh, heh, heh, heh, heh," daring anyone behind him, looking or not, to challenge him, the Vanquisher striding to the side of another of his domains, shrewdly manufacturing it's caste with a kind of innocent joy he gleams to the voyeurs, scene jockeys and jerks there so very entertained...as if the bar had been privy to a joke he played on the dining room...just for them.

Wedging into his perch there, spying Madison Avenue, Albert closes the curtain on the last act, seeding the punctuation with the usual moment of expectant, mischievous calm, a practiced stern face and snap of his cigarette arm in the air to relieve any constriction from his suit sleeve. He plunks his right elbow on the bar – pressing one heel to the frosted glass splash, the dining room behind, left hand pushed against the side of the marble bar top and proceeds to open mouth hack cough what looks like white puss straight at me three or four times. I gratefully watch the projectiles whiz by like torpedoes, employing what diversionary tactics I have developed – flat back against the lowboys – or bowing fast over the sinks of the five foot bar he has entrapped me behind, his fingers gripped around a beverage straw, as he bobs, draining vodka grapefruit after vodka grapefruit, lunch to dinner to close, right elbow planted on the bar-top, locking that forearm straight up – a pearl cufflinked column – supporting the squashed, hot cigarette he clutches stiffly above his bent, sidewinding trajectory of emissions; a gray burning stick he rises to, sucking with obsession between slurps, hacks, rants and lungers.

Out on the terrace, the early diners are gone. The bar starts to get hit from all sides. Raving, champagne indulged brats, dilettante nomads, high rollers priming themselves for a big night and fresh faces – all check in at a bingeing court crammed on sidewalk tables and out into *The Avenue* against a half-circle of stacked limos, all routing business inside, on and surrounding every bar table, waving with one gesticulated weight, oozing Frenchies, over-made broads and ripped regulars, ribs against the bar, to the Maginot Line I hold,

pinched with the rhythm of the cramped crowd's party pulse –
all and every one needing their drink right away, throwing
money at me, pleading, at the same instant that the restaurant
inside has been re-sat and the waiters pound like jail-keepers
for their table's drinks, yelling diving kamikaze through the
thick of it, chest flat over the bar, grabbing bottles of house
wine from my ice and sodas from my sink counter. I am
pirouetting in the three feet separating the bar sinks and the
lowboy refrigerators behind, twirling like a top – slapping my
hands from door handle to bottle neck, shaker to strainer, fruit
pile to ice scoop, can opener to cash drawer, wine coup to water
pitcher, champagne pop to Tropicana carton squeeze – bullshot
to perfect martini – forward – reverse – sideways – forward...
pouring, pouring, pouring – pumping – pumping – pumping,
scribbling unintelligible checks, pulling apart piles of cash, in
the great grabbing swirling whirl – cranking out – raking in –
that this petite bar was *designed* to produce... without a half-
inch to spare.

Near the front of the dining room, Mr. Agnides, the aged
inventor, in the 20's Ramon Navarro's only 'playboy' competition
in Europe and still looking the part, appears to be falling over as
Albert's hand weighs very hard down on the old man's shoulder
with his typical tight grip clamp and wagging head 'Up In Your
Face' encounter, trying to make a point about the decor of some
new club. Mr. Agnide's fading blue eyes spread with anxiety as
Albert piles down even harder for emphasis. "Teece iz no sheik!
Iz buzz stasshhown for two millyon doughlars...Heh! Tease
peeps arrr crrrrasie! Coconaats! Caman, No!"

Albert's trick for the week, always a pretty, white, American,
clean cut boy, has just returned to the bar after a day sleeping
it off at Albert's apartment. Dr. Saadi, very rich, dressing,
veteran V.I.P everywhere, on his third cigarette without a table,
is not impressing his wife, both of them obscured behind the
flower arrangement next to me.

"Ahhh!...Bonsoir Martine...ça va? Come, come...I have
zsumthing nize for you." Into the dining room strides Albert,
holding hands with Martine and her gay lover – skipping – like
kids in a playground. Martine has no reservation, but Albert
has known her since he arrived in America seven years ago, got

130

a job waiting tables at a trattoria across from Bloomies and vowed that he would someday own the chicest bistro in New York and in one amazing segue, three years later, he does. "Alai, Luc! One bottle Veuve Clicquot for Martine!" as he pulls a table out from the wall for them.

"My reservation was for 7:00! We've been standing here for forty minutes! I would like my table!" Dr. Saadi's protest has reached Albert's rabid ear through the roaring grid, "**Ahhhlow!!**" Albert screeches the bar to attention, jerking his cigarette arm high after puffing loudly, rushing back to the bar like he is running to a fight, spitting and woofing all the way. "I haff une kesteaon for you!" jamming himself back in his spot next to me, inflection flying across the bar at the doctor and especially at his wife, "You are doktor, no!?...Eeef I take une appointehehmaant wheat chew, I waaayte in offease, no?!...You wunt to eat now?...**You can waaayte too...O.K.!** Then with the stance and conviction of a Danton, "I am not your slafve!" The privileged cronies rumpled near his side chuckle cruelly as Albert, directing himself, abruptly ends the act most of them have seen before anyway, deferring to his drinking buddies for kudos, having just sacrificed the doctor and his wife for his skit. "Caman no! You go to doktor, you waaayte, no?!...heh, heh, heh, heh, heh."

"Fuck you all!" announces the doctor as loud as he can, before disappearing with his wife out to the next bistro, cafe, trattoria or ristorante nowhere near as hot. As usual, before the night has gotten its bearings, Relais has had its way with it.

Sticking themselves right where the bar begins its loop and the foyer ends are two Black women with big cheap wigs crooked on their heads, long raincoats, carrying large straw bags like you get on 14th St. I know them from when I waited tables in The Village. They would enter Shakespeare's Pub from MacDougal St. side, walk half way through, casing that half of the restaurant, sit down, casing the other half, then snatch a few unguarded purses, splitting quick out the 8th St. side of the joint. I had chased them a few times. These two are well out of their element here. It looks like trouble to me and I am just hoping no one else has noticed them before I have a chance to kick them out. Too late, Dorian has pranced into the dining room, spotted the unlikely clients and stretched his neck back in 'Qu'est-ce que c'est que ça?' pose, thus aiming Albert toward the two ladies.

Encouraging them just past the entrance, where they can all be seen, Albert suddenly halts, in front of them, beginning his vicious, rattling theater – about to become tragic. I see one of the snatchers go into her pocket. I rush out between them, recruiting anyone around to pull Albert away. I back the thieves into the foyer letting them know I remember them. One of them stops me, reaching into her straw bag grabbing hold of something. "I'll blow you away *right now* sucka!" No one is paying attention. Albert is out of the scene and on to some other fiasco as I am stopped speechless, a side show, about to be blown away. "**Huh!** How 'bout I blow yo fuckin' head off right now!" Whipping her hand from the straw bag, she produces a can of 'Aqua Net' hairspray and tries repeatedly to beat me over the head with it as I push them out to the sidewalk, where Luc acknowledges them in the rueful, low, monotone French he speaks to all American's with, thinking they won't respond to what they cannot understand in words. For the next five minutes they pull at his blonde hair, dragging and punching him back and forth across the gaping porthole terrace like a carnival stand target, as the nonplussed crowd calls inside for someone *else* to bring more champagne.

Squat, bearded South American comes by every Saturday with the same routine – limos up – orders "Dom Pérignon, please" {the three English words he can speak} – I pop it – he hands me a $100 bill tip – he drinks half of the bottle very nervously – pays on American Express card that he leaves me a $50 tip on. Everyone in and around the bar is good for at least 5, 10 or 20. I am going to walk out of here with at least $600 tonight... maybe more. Day in – night out – Albert, Albear, Albare – his pranks – his assaults – and *all that money*

It's 1980. Ronald Reagan winnows a blanket of political camouflage over America – promising to end government constraints on the marketplace – tricking the common man into thinking that that might make him a 'Player' – diverting the poor and struggling – the patriotic and naïve – while their pockets are picked clean by raider/junk bond/ hedge fund bandits and armies of their flunkies – drunk with possession – massing and flailing the disposable cash – tempests of repressed aristocratic pipedreams unleashed – all the cocaine, champagne and sex you can buy – 'trickle-down'/'supply-side' lie, quickly exposed in orgies of shameless Gloat – flaunting the stolen millions and billions – as if they were Tribute. Le Relais, *The* Bistro is the absolute playground and court of this engineered windfall – Albert, it's seminal Maître'd.

"Eedeeioat!" "Bete!" "Cretino!" "Bring one *espresso* FAST to Madam Dubonnet – not one *asperreen!*" "Eedeeiot!" "Bete" "Go *Fast!*...Cam on, No!" The new Chinese busboy who doesn't understand English, never mind Albert's comic, spiteful, singular mutation of it, struggles to move faster toward the kitchen as whirs of "Sava" and "Sava Biens" ensue with Victor, the big porn star dealer, trailing in wired with five other Frenchies and their foxes, bearing coke, extruding liberties on me like always – taking with their attitude, great, petty revenge on America for being the hippest place on Earth – for *rock and roll* – for blue jeans – for hamburgers – for blondes – for cowboys – for *courage* – for being the *Empire* this time around – petty revenge, ignoring me completely – except to push their glasses at me for another drink on Albert, while they go on and on and on in the deepest Parisian they can muster, that I do not understand, sticking it to me, a few inches away from my face – signing to the waiters, who pause for brief peeks at my anger and insult as they pass, much too busy to stop – until I am just ready to *walk!* – blocked by Albert planted there against the splash, locking me in – wagging his cigarette, cracking up in my face, enjoying the torture. "One more vodka grapefruit joooze!" ordering me staccato. "Eh, hehe, he, heeeh...," "Peteair...how you like be my slafve Peteair?!" "Heh, heh, heh, heeeeh." He dips smoking into the drink in front of him I have barely had time to refill as the feigning bar percolates for the next episode with affected laughter.

Barbara Walters has just gotten up and is moving directly toward us on her way out, undoubtedly outraged by the nasty display Albert pushed out practically on top of her – as if she is nobody and not the latest and first female network anchor and the restaurant has nothing to fear from the word of her mouth or her comment which I am sure is about to commence – maybe even a *smack* for Albert – who pop turns like he has eyes behind his head, cutting her off as she reaches the bar, "Madam Walltear, I hope you dun't mind joke...isss only joke...I hope I nut disturb you," he entreaties, head tilted in supplication doggy style, persuasion switched way on with instant impish smile and showers of goggling sincerity, grabbing her hand in both of his and tugging down like an old friend, till she blushes, face to heels, disarmed and charmed by Albert, his arcane speech and fearless gall – succumbing to the Alchemy of Audacity, the spell of the Bistro Myth and the attentions of its Bacchus.

Barbara Walters will be back and the schmoozing sacrifice will continue through the bruising decadence of the early 80's, Albert, testing drug and drug, club and club, New York, Rio, Paris, St. Tropez, Miami, St. Barts, every night, libertine appetite wailing past daylight – gay tricks from filthy basement to palace gate, Riviera bungalow to Hudson River dock, flying his banner of promiscuity high – pioneering Excess as The Mode – while the world keeps throwing us Big Bucks enough to support it in style, there on Madison Avenue with the doors wide open.

Albert reproduces the show he puts on using anyone who happens to be standing there, because he knows it's the sadistic thing his audience likes – and it's good business – these parts we play – the drinks he buys – the food he buys – this foul circus he barks ring to ring, cursing all the way, tossing insult after insult at anyone he knows will take it – and that's most everybody – for as long as they can take it – except those he knows he must pay solemn, ass licking obeisance to – and that's good business also –

        good business limousine'd after hours to every club, every night, his bad behavior getting much worse on display before a drifting high society out for a good time, where his unflinching nastiness offers up to them a constant spark, elevating him to living legend in that protected circle so dumb lamed by disco and coke –

good business when he returns every morning at 11:30 to his spot at the bar still smoking, for two strong espressos getting him going for another rout – and whatever happens, shameless, hilarious, frightening, enticing, offensive, inspiring, is good business for him, owning, inch for inch, the most profitable restaurant on Earth –

good business for all of us – busboy to Maître d' – going home with $300, or 4, or 6...or $1,000...

good business after closing, parking himself on the little corner sidewalk table closest to the entrance – reveling, goofing on the Eurotrash, the chippies, the fags, the famous and everyone else – the whole scene and everybody in it – as if he is one of *us* – puffing away wickedly, as the wheel screws a little closer to the dynamic of this phenomena – Relais – Albert – his rude madness – and the insinuation of something deeply French.

... ...

I am still in the neighborhood, now managing a place with two more "stars"' than Relais...heh! – almost acclimated to a normal income. It's been years since I dared walk past Relais. It's too painful. Mortified by how I let myself go with cocaine there, embarrassed by the breakdowns I went through trying to find a steady job after I left there – threatened by the loneliness of any other restaurant compared to Relais – with Albert close next to me erupting and endearing himself to me, despite ourselves. I am afraid of those faces out on the terrace or at the bar still partying. Their eyes might point me out. I was the fool they saw throw it all away. And after all the money, all the business, all the parties, all the clubs, all the people, I am left with not one connection to it all...not even Albert. The only time I laid eyes on him in the five years since I left was once. Rambling across 63rd St., The Maître of all the Laughter and all the Dying that Relais had seen, as drugs and A.I.D.S. killed off the 80's party. Ironic thing was, the ones who could most afford the party were the first to go. I didn't call to Albert as he passed by that day. I had to drop him and the whole fantastic Relais chapter, as dry and deserted as things had become, to find a new life – one I could survive.

I've reached 60th St. Four o'clock. I'm shaking my head, flashing back on Relais at 4 p.m...just about the time the night begins with a few tall quiet types at the bar trying to be cool, the terrace tables are being snatched up like musical chairs by usual suspects staking out that afternoon's batch of beauties passing by, foreigners from all over the map lining up inside to feel as close to New York City by way of Paris as they can, sucking down Kir Royale and Pastis automatically as rush hour fumes billow from grid-locked buses a few feet away...a waiter and a bartender left to deal with the largesse, a half hour after the last lunch guest has split. I can picture it exactly. I feel the tension set in. I am sparked again by the excitement of Relais. I pass Maxim's. I still have time to cross the street or go to back to Fifth Avenue, but this time, I don't.

Past the Relais clones and galleries turned luggage stores and department boutiques, I cross 63rd on the west side of Madison toward Le Relais's terrace, now a mere thirty feet away. At the very last table before the entrance – the corner table – Albert's table – sits a deeply tanned man whose nearly formless face looks like an unwrapped mummy just returned from Copacabana Beach. His eyes, the only thing left with shape on his head, jut macabre from the bag of dark skin they are set in. As I come closer, I am drained of pulse for a second – stricken by a ghost... the ghost of a whirlwind that still fills me with repulsion and exhilaration, melancholy and fear – the inspiration and culmination of what now seems to me a lost chapter – in this moment – barely yet undeniably identified by a sole marker –

elbow cocked straight up from that table, pumping and squeezing a weathered cigarette, Albert The Terrible, who would eat you for lunch; Albert The Mad Merlin, who kept the Soirée alive – plopped down at that corner table scanning the Boulevard, just like always, only now, wrecked with A.I.D.S., a few weeks from dying out there on Madison Avenue with the doors wide open.

1956

last Fall
I started with
3 fairly common drugs
prescribed
for fairly
common conditions
– good for the survival
doctor sez –

last Winter I
thought I found
a good place to pee
during The Sopranos
or some other show
I was hooked on
still keeping my eye
on the T.V.

I also imagined
that the pachysandra
outside my sunroom
would benefit
from steady irrigation

it died

to the root

following these results
and feeling a bit suspicious,
I picked three places
on the lawn
just to see
if my hunch
was correct.

Now, in summer height,
there are three dead spots
in the lawn...
those three exactly.

well, if I were a young,
enterprising bloke
from Bangalore
or Northern California
or the Curie I always
pictured myself,

I might create whole cloth
from these discoveries
and stop the world
with a new way to eliminate
suburban sprawl,
or wash dishes without water,
or keep camels
from crapping on your chest

...but these days
I just stand and stare
– Cowboy Hat Tall –
at the burn-holes
in the grass –

transfixed
by the afternoon
'Hound Dog'
arrived at
my record shop
on South Orange Avenue
just north of 9th Street

Easter Acid Braised Lamb Shanks Moroccan

Ingredients:

4 local baby lamb shanks
Raz el Hanout spice rub
garlic
cilantro
Rosé du Provence
dried figs
dried cherries
tangerine
honey
bay leaf
hot pepper flakes
olive oil
Kosher salt
flour

... ...

Lay shanks out on flat platter.
smash 4 cloves of garlic,
rub into each shank thoroughly,
pressing harder where meat is exposed,
until garlic's oil begins to penetrate

rub each shank thoroughly
with spice mix for 3 or
4 minutes until spices
begin to penetrate

cover shanks with
plastic wrap.
refrigerate.

retire for the evening
Lullabied by Disney
Morning Glory Chefchaouen Reverie:
kitchen-shack Mustafa
tipping open his pot tops like lockets
to grandfathered treats of meat,
vegetable and spice for your ten cents
choice at longhair long table
bound for oud/drum
Kif House blackout farewells
to their labyrinthed
blue/pink stucco pastel
mountainside village
on last night before truck
up into The Atlas...

a pilot's dream
a wonderwall
a joker's dust
Fatima's Call

... ...

rise refreshed

remove shanks from
refrigerator.
discard garlic pieces from meat,
sprinkle with more spice rub
rub each shank with ½ teaspoon
Kosher salt.

dredge each shank thoroughly
in sifted white flour.

in a warm roasting pan
heat 5 tablespoons
olive oil

brown shanks on all sides

remove shanks from pot

add 8 crushed garlic cloves,
½ teaspoon of hot pepper seeds
and 1 Turkish bay leaf to pot.
cook until garlic begins to color.

add 10 oz. Rosé du Provence to pot
turn up heat and deglaze,
reducing wine by ⅓.

Stir in 1 tablespoon honey an
½ teaspoon Kosher salt

add 4 dried Turkish figs halved,
a dozen dried cherries, ½ tangerine
(not squeezed) and
6 sprigs of fresh cilantro tied.

Cook for 3 minutes.

Add shanks back to pot.

Cover and place into oven
pre-heated to 250 degrees.

brush off excess spice rub
from hands

Go to large sunlit room.

Do the Flip, Flop, Flail
And Fly Hippie Hippie Shake,
making sure hands
wave spice aromas
like incense,
while being careful not
to touch furniture.

When dizzy, lay stomach up, eyes
shut, on flat floor, as aromas begin
to escape from oven...

fall out,..

... ...

suddenly upside-down
dropping headfirst like a bomb

Ourfatherwhoartinheaven
hallowedbethynamethy
kingdomcomethywillbedone
onearthasitisinheaven

I figure if I can get up
and walk away after I
hit, it'll be a miracle...
I am comfortable with
miracles...

giveusthisdayourdailybread
andforgiveusourtrespasses
asweforgivethosewhotrsepass
againstus

I am calm
I am aware that I am calm...
if this is it – this is it –

andleadusnotintotemptation
butdeliverusfromevil

still falling

Ourfatherwhoart
inheavenhallowedbethyname

I had my fun...never expected
to live past 20 anyway

thykingdomcome
thywillbedone
onearthasitisinheaven

no complaints
I got out...

I had my kicks...
I caught that ticket
to Paradise...

giveusthisdayourdailybread
andforgiveusourtrespasses
asweforgivethosewhotrespass
againstus

still falling now seeing

Gibraltar Straits
to Old Tangier, gold lit
necklace of long twilight Africa,
genie breeze plume swift mystery
jalabaed droop-eye motif
disappears watching inside
smoked corner hills over-packed
donkeys timpani waddle up
into Casbah Symphony bazaar roar
minaret wail swirl, split
second silences floating canvas,
then quick slamming back to
street of dreams I can smell...
Up The Hill
Up The Hill
For 5,000 Years
Up The Hill
To The Medina

10,000 sparrows
swarm sunset
we ride out – 'Marrakesh
Express' – 4 months gone
from Amsterdam – across
Barbary Coast, south to Ketama,
Fez, Chefchaouen, The Atlas,
Essaouira, Marrakesh, Agadir to
Taghazout Beach...

still falling

andleadusnotintotemptation
butdeliverusfromevil

Up The Hill
Up The Hill
Find Me Forever
Up The Hill
To The Medina

by the time flashback stops
(about 3 hours),
meat will be falling off of the bone

wash hands thoroughly
remove pot from oven

Marvel
that you once went off
a pitch black night 150 foot
cliff onto Sahara beach floor
and rose without a scratch.

let set until company arrives

Wild Weekend

I am tall tree in its branches reflected on Dal Lake. The moon shines full behind me, night clouds sailing between us, configuring motion and wind: light shuttered – refracted – then exposed by my waving limb arms above the water that has captured this vivid locket alluring contemplation, as the pilgrim approaches its banks.

Jaw sore grind ache down neck head roll whip like dead into aisle – the ghost of embarrassment interrupting mouth open drooled trance – like always – must be New Paltz. Wiggle up in my seat – plant brain base back to headrest, pursuing faint dream cover enforcing privacy on cramp sat, rustled newspaper, allergy victim, CB static, close air Trailways bus.

Inside and stretching the perimeter of a rectangle courtyard swarmed with maroon robed monks and incense, three levels of wooden balconies bow with the weight of big gold hat lamas stiff in their places, shoulder to shoulder solemn over anxious crowd below now shoving and shouting as the ground beneath them begins to flutter. The balconies ripple with the cries – the lamas do not respond. I have seen this before...in America...in France...in China – high imagining themselves mighty. I see my naiveté, thinking that it can't happen here, in The Monastery...in Tibet.

I run up unnoticed through the balconies. The building begins shaking and twisting. I climb the stairways, jumping steps through the second – then to the top balcony – everything creaking and swaying. I reach the side of the head lama. I study his face like a map, memorizing his ugly folly, arrogant to the end. The balcony cracks, then crumbles, imploding in one great plume of dust, incense and fire.

145

Shift down globe/circle curve Kingston Thruway exit/long tilt right signal to open eyes shut safe from intrusion since Port Authority – repeating 10 year re-entry ritual this bus provides me in decelerating spirals...like I am an astronaut...or a seeker. Shuffling of arrival waves chatter through the cabin, now animated with 'Weekender' anticipation. Relieved by each familiar indication, I straighten my back for balance – as a right turns onto 375, direct line of sight to hulking Great Spirit Overlook Mountain cradling downtown Woodstock, whose long side I am dropped at, alone at the top of my hill – bus wiping in front of me; across me with its 'Trailways' logo, cargo bay, faces I almost know, blue-gray dimmed in their seats for other stops – the coach now growling up Mill Hill with last black exhaust blowing Big Apple reminder.

One block from my hermitage, peace is animated each step down the hill. My pilgrimage to contemplation enters itself in early evening dance down that hill, choreographed primal in Muse configured by glint of star form, cloud roll and moon dare. I walk looking up, releasing protection, forgiving need and joining stillness in trail of enunciation to my door.

Retrieving this secret with each visit, I sanctify land and home with gratitude. Slow-slow, detailing a symphony with a whisper, inside the wing of screened porch studio, surrounded in tree walls, here for months, re-taking as I write, every footstep of ten thousand first time walked, just to see where the path leads, from Gamru-Tika up the back side of mountain – to surprise end in the Dalai Lama's compound – 30 years ago –
every step impossible to recreate – yet, I do – and keep moving. I shudder, revisiting heights buried – just in case I survived Surviving in NYC. Each move, each turn, distilled quiet of disturbance – left being there on that trail of lotus and smoke, where ancient trees reach over high peak horizon. I wind up goat trail/turning path, as close to Tibet as it can get...

A first sight shock as I round a bend – dragon rushed color mandala implant, Dharma labels bright – *The Tibetan School* – abruptly set – ready or not – into mountain bluff, giant horns outside pointed over valleys and plains –

a thousand stone steps behind
lead me to the Dalai Lama's
residence – branding humility on
my no Buddhist but lucky ass to
have ever taken that walk.

I am finishing that chapter
ending back
at The Tibetan School
        blocked decades

– now given to the treasure
given me –
                I revisit,
                        awake to the Dalai Lama's greeting,
                        his humor adept,
                        his blessing
                        as I left –
                        nature co-operating
                        in formal lesson –
                        answering each of my questions
                        full display –
                        lifted by the clarity
                        and exhilaration of Arrival

I lay claim to impending solitude, stepping toward my studio,
across a living room Dylan once drove his motorcycle through,
around a corner from a shack they say Van Morrison composed
'Moondance' and 'Tupelo Honey' in...my long ride will now be
crowned with work...perhaps I will complete my tribute to the
great monk and his people tonight...

                        Everything offensive and all as
                        nasty nasty loud as it can get right
                        behind me over a fence jam
                        slamming loose pieces break
                        breaking bad records scratched
                        with skunk paws till creeps pop up
                        whenever they feel like – in my face
                        with very unwelcome jive insisting
                        how bad and tough they are, these

little and big fat bourgeois pussies
in Mercedes, gambling en vogue
posse cover against sold out lives
selling as fast as their rap, tonight
raved by White college kids frat
drunk 'muthafuckin' – 'bitch' – 'yo yo
yo!' masking mental vacancy with
new cool blitherings between fake
laugh eruptions nailed to their lame
act in suburbia, where they hip-
hopped here from in the expensive
sneaks, wagged hats and baggy
pants, ass crack view vogue –
pumping WORD where there is no
melody – framed in lockup out of
affluence these skinny white punks
making noise take for granted
        and now disturb my
collecting mind – ridiculing
their own selves in the very
text singing along, where
there is no song, redundance
clips hashed out on streets
they dare not walk, by cross
armed flare nostril armies
promised to desperation by
color.

Rap...butch Disco sister, bravado-wrapped no bite all bark dog
of envy, servicing national threat fetish with hip pretense
buffoons before a decade fast forward trying too little too late to
convalesce from itself with cleverness mock masochist set up
for 'Y2K' clamp down, in screening room sat with 'industry'
bean counters, thumbs stuck way up all the way to the bank.

Rap...thirty feet away, tarring me.

Rap...I can't hear myself...I can't think....

Rap...my perfect neighbor must have given her place up for the
weekend to these little jerks I am about to confront and shut
down...

148

Till I catch myself caught,
distracted from rage
            long and loud enough
            to notice myself
            about to pull a trigger
            on a gun of intolerance...
                    long and loud enough
                    to stop me, stepping back
                            to when I was
                            the "too much"
                            target...
                releasing me
                fed back
                to
                how
                hip happy sad
                I was
                when the world
                was on *my* shoulders
                            blasting...

                    ... ...

Rocking chair snatch womb entitlement sudden distributes free
love to all willing to smile on fast tracks of guitar victory and
poetry exalted to common understanding, knitting feedback and
flowers into banners spotted waving above family, nation and
mountain, across a country caught off guarding limitation with
persecution, while the class of the 60's dissolves matter to mind
first hand, in unison contact high, its collective middle finger
flicked in the face of all conformity, sparing no one barefoot
naked brazen intrusion, attracting consciousness toward space
enough to destroy anything unkind – easy – simply willing it.

Entrance to that moment demanded passion – order turned on its
head by conscription to the very arms high over head push,
volunteer peeling a planet layer of consciousness, rolling it up like
an old carpet, till jettisoned garbage with cheers to Rebel

Sentinels who cut open epoch gates, calling us to crash with
urgency the party of Mind and take reigns in administering its
promise to Surrender and Become, because it is _supposed_ to
be...en masse...right now, not later.

And when we had succeeded with the manual installation of an
Age, all Cause, all Fervor suddenly moderated before our
Achievement and there was nothing left to do but sit back, watch
and suffer the epiphany theater of a culture dead with Society,
romanced with denial, failing in pieces through our lifetime, as
the prophesy of even our most daring efforts is reflected by the
mechanics of a world inching in fits and restarts straight to the
Human Be-In.

The music, still playing, was as loud as it took to entertain a
World Arc, navigating technological floods while simultaneously
blown open by Contextuality itself. The music, still playing, was
as soft as it could be, to speak the uncompromising emotion of
Transformation.

... ...

O.K. kids! Where and how do I come off shutting you down?
My youth did not educate me that way.

I write through the night, through the serial nerve splitting
cat/hack cacophony, now inspiring me with its 'gap,' like an old
friend there with me sharing a laugh about another gap...and
long after the rap babies have turned in – then out – of their
logoed cradles and begun the noise again,

> I have outlined every player, from sky to lotus,
> above Gamru-Tika,
> down the mountain this time –
>
> to The Tibetan School,
>
> where I sit on a long stoop
> there on Buddha Street.

I complete my draft. I jump! I breathe. I run. I shake. I don't know what to do. I take my old bike out and around the corner, where Overlook Mountain stops me overwhelmed – orange/red 3,000 foot mound of beauty in best autumn day blue sky sunshine glory. Marilyn passes on her old bike, happy to see me out of the house. I rent a car to ride us to Overlook mountaintop for the first time.

Woodstock fall is peak
Evergreens squeeze bursting vista
yellow, red, butterscotch and high

I lean between breaths of rush
while summer goes,
now freeing, flying,
falling with leaves
turning exhilaration
landing life beads

gliding up the mountain
racing in color spray
reminded of who
we are and
and when we first met
and had no time
for anything but us,
Released
by this mountain,
on Hail wheels
lost to the road
to the top,
I expect only to get there
when we swerve 'round
a bunch of tall trees –
shedding golden/red
Escher veil
to sudden wind
turning left to the summit –

Marilyn waves her arm, "Look!"

and out across some grass,

there it is

The Tibetan School...

perched without warning again

vivid and dazzling,
abrupt and austere
as it was
a world away
a quarter of a life ago,
just up the mountain

one
more
time
ready
or not
one
more
time

... ...

Way Under Overlook now, Holy Green Bus Stop Dead Book prep
line Sunday bags me flapping Future Blue like always...but this
time still full circle satisfied from finally been to fool on hill Tibet
school I never knew was there before, that I now see clear stuck
up on high horizon, over tall lean Methodist steeple pointing it
out a mark from Tinker Street.

I know where I am going. Back where I came...and that's
alright...it's O.K...

*...radio tweeter shriek hollers RAP very annoying and
Unintelligible, I.D.'d from this year's "Free Tibet" concert by the
true freak kid boom-box sat down now right behind me on
concrete steps...and it's alright...it's O.K....*

152

Hey! Beastie Boy lama-like crop top
Pop 'Lollapalooza' exposure
all you
Hollywood Hunks
'Kun Dun'
'Seven Years In'
old fashioned Genghis media blitz,
again preferring Shambala to confession...

Tasha Dalek!

...the coaches pull up like duct tape – rash...
one for Kingston
...one for New York City.

downtown Woodstock
1999

Empty Hallway

ceiling pock
old bed
pajama race
tree blink
stocking dig
paper rip
box pop
plastic rattle
metal grind
feet pound
floor creak

shoe shine
cufflink
passed-on suit
new tie
ancient pin
Brylcreem
brim hat

stone church
hard kneel
mass song

picture near stoop

granma
granpa
salutation
goomba
gooma
papa
mama
dialect explosion

kids sit
other room
card table
child princess
child jerk
dressed to kill

skadole soup
antipasto
raviola
meatball
braciole
sausage sweet
sausage hot

green salad
whole bird
5 vegetable

fruit crunch
nut crack
fennook

t.v. men
crazy kids
women dish

coffee
espresso
ricotta pie
cake
pumpkin pie
biscotti
honey twist
butter cookie
sugar cookie
struvela
macaroon

men sleep t.v.
women dish
kids hide

Sinatra
King Cole
menthe
cacao
anisette
espresso
anisette cookie

good night paisan

pajama
Scrooge
Scrooge
late Scrooge
tree off
good night

Gone
Gone
all Gone
along with
the agita

Cuvee Amber

Old Pilgrim
Arms High
To Sun Translucent

Baking Up Storms
Across Great Plains
Of Moment

Old Pilgrim

Sweeping Out
Gestalt
Swept Under
Experience Rugs

Drying Rock
Sand And Pebble
Of Emotion
In Cool Breeze
Full Display

Shoe
And Hat
Removed
For Warmth

Old Pilgrim
Takes The Day

Balls Big
As Moon

nice as Nice

rushing tatters of late July
stuffed rags of August
tumble of leaves and sky
hickory
stone
mercy
fear
eggs
melon

      – brown/gray/green
      chalk smoke veil
      burning off Tinker Street –

Sun, better than yesterday...
quiet cool steam...
guitar strum
'just like a ringin' a bell'
keeps Woodstock popping,
clean of cut
and nice as Nice
in thought and Feeling of Sun...

Sun in frame of touch
and memory –
motion and reflection –
time and honesty

Sun Sunbrag of Day –
– every one –
in downtown valley
bright with brand: Redemption –

while fly-hi Lenape Chief
shouldering Overlook Mountain
dreams us a look
or 2...or 3
at dirt
and gravel
and steel
of Sundance
in heat of Self
gone fire of Self
under virgin Sun

no other

When We Get Old
(to Marilyn)

---

when we get old
I want a piggy-back

when we get old
I'll wear my Soul Shoes

when we get old
the trees will be
fatter and taller
and down

there will be different birds
in the neighborhood
(I hope the crows don't come back)

when we get old
I will see your face
just like it is today
and your sweet favor
the blessing
of my life

when we get old
cars will be wings –
music thought
and every sandwich
breakfast

we'll keep our legs
elevated every chance
worries set to rest
Kindness its own reward
words rarely used

when we get old
our differences
won't matter
trouble seldom
money scarce
vision repaired
feelings channeled
and seasons still
change

when we get old
I will smell your cooking
in the backyard
pumping into
a breeze
and I will disappear
even less
if that is possible

The Feast of Saint Rocco

Grandpa
Called My Mother
To His Side
As He Lay Dying In Bed
– Only Her –
Like Some Sort
Of Sacrimony

I Saw Him
Whisper Direction
In Old Sicilian

And Then He Died

I Think
It Was
All About
Me
And The Birth Curse
Of My 'Veil'
And The Problem
Of My Autism

Because He Knew
Of The Beatings
The Ropes
The Paddles
The Straps

The Isolation
The Betrayals
The Heartbreak
And The Banishment

And He Knew Me –
The Quiet Little Kid
Who Got A Nickel
Off Him –
Drawn From
His Left Vest Pocket –
Every Time
I Saw Him –
In Faithful Dispensations
Of A Trust
That I Would
Survive
The Brutalities
Of Superstition

I Drink This Water
In Grandpa's Wine

VAGABOND